LIGHT RAIL AND
HEAVY POLITICS

"You don't have to trust the trolley company
in order to let it take you where you want to go."

Tom Wolfe, *Man in Full*

Jack McCroskey

TENLIE
PUBLISHING

ISBN 0-9729227-0-9

Printed in the United States of America

TENLIE PUBLISHING
Denver, CO 80209

Cover Art, Design and Book Layout by Stephanie Hill
(www.stephill.com)

First Printing: March 2003

10 9 8 7 6 5 4 3 2 1

ACKNOWLEDGMENTS

For their much needed help in editing and producing this book, I want to thank: Barry Clements, Elizabeth Colatrella, Nancy Deutsch, Frank Fitch, Ted Gleichman, Stephane Hill, Gloria Holliday, Jim Krendl, Jack Phinney, Jerry Powell, Leigh Rich, Kevin Sampson, Andre Ransom, Cameron Winder and Bill Womack.

I also want to thank my family—not just for their help, but mainly for their enduring patience in listening to me ramble on and on about light rail and heavy politics year after year and even decade after decade: Bettye, Mark and Jacquelyn, Thomas and Marilyn, Marissa and Tenlie, Maura and John.

To my beautiful wife Bettye.
Thanks for a lifetime of love and kindness.

CONTENTS

ILLUSTRATIONS

1
OVERVIEW
When, Where, How and Who of Denver Light Rail

When did light rail arrive in Denver? Who plopped it down in the middle of the city? Where did the start-up money come from? Why were so many citizens so zealously opposed? How did its supporters manage to emerge triumphant? What can other communities learn from Denver?

Questions like these deserve thoughtful answers. The quality of urban mobility—both in the here-and-now and during the long-term future—will depend in large part on how thoroughly citizens understand the issues.

In this volume we explore these matters in a historical context, which hangs together much better than a strictly contemporary view, but which also takes somewhat longer. One reason for the additional length is that history goes back practically forever and that chronicles venturing anywhere near ground zero have a lot of territory to cover. For example:

Norman Davies launches his magisterial *Europe, A History* (1996) about 40,000 years ago during the ice ages.[1] He continues through human settlement and goes on to nation-building and industrialization. He continues with World Wars I and II and concludes with excursions into the Cold War. Closer to home, Fred Anderson in *Crucible of War* (2000) claims it's practically impossible to understand the American Revolution without a reading acquaintance of the French and Indian War (1754-66).[2] Otherwise, he persuasively argues, there is no appreciating how early battle lines were drawn or why the Americans eventually won.

Contemplating these truly compelling examples, the author found himself briefly tempted to preface this study with a sightseer's ramble through the birth and early childhood of the wheel. BUT FEAR NOT, VALUED READERS. DO NOT CLOSE THIS BOOK. THERE IS NO LINGERING DISPOSITION HERE TO DO ANYTHING OF THE SORT.

There are several good reasons why not. For one, the author is not a professional historian. He is rather a practicing economist who has worked the highways and byways of state-and-local government for some 25 years. What's more, he is now entering what novelist John O'Hara calls "Waiting for Winter"—the stage of life in which stamina declines and the need for downtime begins to rise.[3]

This story will therefore start in the recent past (comparatively speaking) at the time of the invention of public transport in New York City during the 1820s. It proceeds through the evolution of public-transport vehicles—from omnibuses, horsecars and cable cars to trolleys, trams, streetcars and light rail.

The glory decades when trams and trolleys ruled the urban scene will be covered, as will their subsequent fall to near extinction. Turning to the why and wherefore of this near-death experience, we focus on analysis of government discrimination and on predatory attacks by Big Autos and Big Oil. General Motors played the major role in this restraint of trade. But as novelist Don DeLillo has asked about the lies General Motors tells: What's to be done? "We need the cars."

From here the narrative moves to the wholesale shift during the 1950s and '60s from private ownership to government control. Marking a major watershed nationally in public-transport history, the transfer took place in Denver in 1969. This evolution and creation of the Denver Regional Transportation District (RTD) led to years of acrimonious debate apropos the most suitable sort of governance: an appointed board or an elected board. When voters opted for the latter as the result of a citizen initiative, the stage was set for huge breakthroughs along the light-rail front—

notably the building of the original segment, the 5.3-mile Metro Area Connection (MAC) through downtown Denver and adjacent neighborhoods.

Many premature critics, speaking out before the MAC got underway, regaled the project as "the line to nowhere." "Ain't nobody want it," some neighborhood activists chanted. "Ain't nobody going to ride it." These voices have long since been drowned out by the surge of eager passengers.

Opening during early fall 1995, amidst whirlwind festivities and widespread applause, the MAC was believed by many residents to be Denver's first electric-powered, rail-based public transport. Actually, it was the third. The first appeared in 1885, a short-lived experimental line that fizzled soon after opening. The second experienced a 60-year life span, beginning in 1890 and lasting until 1950.

The MAC differs from these two in more than updated technology and creative public financing. Most substantially it was planned from the outset as a stalemate-breaking way of getting tracks on the ground with trains running along them. It was likewise intended as the core segment of a regional system and also as a demonstration of rail's day-to-day utility and acceptability.

Three additional segments have already been approved and funded. The first added 8.7 track miles in July 2000; the others will add 21.4 more miles when completed. At this writing the total system is more than 35 track miles in length, either in operation or under construction.

Confounding early critics who foresaw empty seats and public indifference giving birth to a hungry herd of snow-white elephants, the system has consistently attracted many more riders than expected. Nor have feared budgetary upheavals erupted—although the economic slowdown beginning in 2001 has underscored the ongoing need for cost-effectiveness in all RTD operations.

The author wraps up his account of Denver's continuing light-rail saga with the following opinion: This time, the third time around, will prove the charm. The MAC will grow bigger and last longer than its predecessors. These aren't shoo-in predictions of course. Predictions concerning projects of such magnitude and distance seldom are. But the prospects look bright and will take on klieg-light intensity if two reforms can be successfully completed.

First, the MAC's long-term value depends on resolution of the struggle between two competing strategies. One, which has been demonstrated by failed elections as the pragmatically and politically weaker, is the notion that RTD must build out light rail all at once with a correspondingly big hike in sales taxes. The author believes the stronger strategy—in Denver as in many other jurisdictions during this period of fiscal stringency—lies in building the system incrementally, with no immediate tax increases. This latter approach has worked well thus far, and without it Denver today would have nothing at all in the way of rail. Interestingly enough there is a historical precedent for moving incrementally.

During the late 1850s the US Congress stood poised to fund the route necessary to complete a transcontinental railroad from the existing railroad head in Omaha through Nebraska, Wyoming, Utah and Nevada on to a terminus in Sacramento, California. But action was blocked by sectional jealousies. Dixie legislators wanted a route along the country's southern borders into San Diego and pushed for simultaneous authorization and construction. The issue could not be resolved until secession and the Civil War when Confederate-minded senators and representatives withdrew to below the Mason-Dixon Line. With President Lincoln's enthusiastic urging, the US House of Representatives then passed the Pacific Railroad Bill in May 1862 by a vote of 79 to 49; the Senate accepted the measure by 35 to 5 that June. Ultimately other transcontinental routes were constructed but one can reasonably conclude that the second and third routes could not have come to pass without the first.

The author also believes we need a vigorous shake-up in

RTD's top bureaucracy. RTD's current crew seems to have signed on mainly to acquire overpriced real estate, take credit for other people's labors and boost ever higher their already lofty earnings. In terms of public policy, this problem opens wide the gate for light-rail opponents. Bureaucratic overreaching and nest-feathering are scarcely the way to burnish one's image, let alone win citizen backing.

Before moving into the chronicle itself, the author would like to pause just a moment and make one final comment about this business of "Waiting for Winter." Pretty obviously life's later years can entail pain and problems. The author himself suffers a creeping inability to climb trees. Fortunately, however, there is an upside. Hanging around watching clouds drift by and pondering seasonal changes leaves one totally free to call things by their proper names.

And what is the rightful name for RTD's recent purchase of Denver's ramshackle Union Station for $50 million when a fair market price would have run closer to $5 million?[4] "A fraud on the public," that's what—a fraud perpetrated under the dark shadow of constitutional transgressions, including the deliberate denial of board members' civil rights and free speech.

We ventilate these offenses in the penultimate chapter and address our continuing efforts to send such authoritarian maneuvers back to where they came from . . . specifically, back to the long-ago era before Americans enjoyed the freedoms proclaimed by the First Amendment to the US Constitution.

Notes

1. Norman Davies, *Europe, A History*, Oxford [England]; NY; Oxford University Press, 1996.
2. Fred Anderson, *Crucible of War: The Seven Years' War and the Fate of Empire in British North America, 1754-1766*, NY; Alfred A. Knopf; Distributed by Random House, 2000.
3. John O'Hara, *Waiting For Winter*, [Stories], NY; Random House, 1966.
4. Voting yes were: Chairwoman Mary Blue (District I), Bob Briggs (District J), Bill Elfenbein (District A), Carl Erickson (District E), Rick Garcia (District C), Dick McLean (District O), Stephen Millard (District M), Wallace Pulliam (District L), O'Neill P. Quinlan (District G), David E. Rose (District K), David Richman (District M), Bob Tonsing (District H), Jim Zavist (District D). Voting no: Rosemary Paolillo (District F). Abstaining: Gloria Holliday (District B).

2

PRIVATELY OWNED PUBLIC TRANSPORT
From Cobblestones to Rails to Overhead Wires

Already a kaleidoscope of horses and mules and harried pedestrians mixed with a melange of carts and carriages, the streets of New York City witnessed in 1827 the beginnings of a new approach to personal mobility. Businessman Abraham Brower, who owned stables in lower Manhattan at 667 Broadway, brought to life the idea of public transport—that is, urban transportation along specified routes at specific times. Cabs and hacks had trolled the area for years, it is true, but these lacked the regularity and predictability Brower envisioned.

The new reality manifested itself as a two-horse carriage carrying 10 to 12 riders in two separate compartments. Brower called his creation the "Accommodation." A similar conveyance, absent the compartments, hit town one year later. Passengers sat in hip-to-hip proximity on benches running the entire length of the vehicle. This rig Brower aptly dubbed the "Sociable."

The Accommodation and the Sociable soon evolved into more capacious coaches. Originating in the venues of Paris and London where introduced by George Shillibeer, a British citizen and former seaman, these grand conveyances seemed positively huge by prevailing standards. Known generically as "omnibuses," they seated up to 20 passengers.

Gaudily painted and individually named after luminaries such as George Washington and Alexander Hamilton, omnibuses gained almost immediate favor—with more than 100 soon navigating up and down and around Manhattan. As Charles Dickens wrote of Broadway: "No stint of omnibuses here! Half a dozen have gone by within as many minutes. Plenty of hackney cabs and coaches too: gigs, phaetons, large-wheeled tilburies and private carriages . . . Black and white coachmen in straw hats, black hats, white hats, glazed caps, fur caps; in coats of drab, black, brown, green, blue, mankeen, striped jean and linen."[1] Before long the phenomena spread to other cities, including Philadelphia, Boston and Baltimore.

Creating Controversy

Patronage posed no problem. Horse-drawn omnibuses were convenient, reliable and relatively cheap—more expensive than shank's mare but much less than hiring hacks or keeping carriages. Even so, they soon generated controversy. From riders' point of view, omnibuses became possibly too popular—overcrowded and occasionally rowdy. They were also sweltering in summer and brutally cold in winter and when banging over cobblestone streets could cause discomfort and even spinal dislocations.

From the viewpoint of other drivers, a looming omnibus portended trouble. Omnibus drivers were accused of hogging the road and of cutting into and out of traffic. They liked, claimed the critics, to menace hacks and gigs and other light coaches—and sometimes they tried to squash them. "A ferocious spirit," said the *New York Herald*, "appears to have taken possession of omnibus drivers, which defies law and delights in destruction." The paper doubtlessly exaggerated. (One of the few constants in the mostly checkered history of public transport is the media's tendency to magnify industry shortcomings, whether real or make-believe.)

Horse-Cars

But while complaints were overstated, improvements were nonetheless sorely wanted. This need was met partly by putting horse-drawn omnibuses on railroad tracks, thereby moving from wooden wheels on cobblestones to iron wheels on metal rails.

The public named the new prodigies "horse-cars."

America's first horse-car line opened in New York City during 1832 under the aegis of John Mason, a wealthy banker and merchant. It ran one mile between Prince and 14th Streets along Fourth Avenue, with another three miles being added over the next several years. At almost the same time a similar line started in New Orleans. More than six miles long, it shuttled from Canal Street to suburban Carrolton. (The service continues today and is known as the "St. Charles Streetcar.")

Overcoming Opposition

But horse-cars didn't proliferate as rapidly as omnibuses. Why the delay? One reason: Home and business owners along proposed alignments often opposed construction, contending developments could create a nuisance and lower property values. But once lines began to operate opinions usually changed. Word soon circulated that horse-cars were in actuality quiet, smooth, commodious and generally supportive of property prices.

Another problem: Early rails consisted of wrought-iron strips on wooden stringers. These protruded four inches and more above street level, creating hazards for other vehicles. An improved steel rail became available during the early 1850s (one that allowed a fairly flush street surface) and for the next generation horse-cars ruled public transport. By the beginning of the Civil War in 1861 systems operated in established cities such as Boston, Charleston, Philadelphia, Pittsburgh, Cincinnati and Chicago.

In many newer towns out West horse-cars started up as soon as populations warranted. Colorado's Territorial Government granted a charter to the Denver Horse Railroad Company in 1867 when Denver was little more than a village. Five years later horse-cars rolled along Larimer, Champa and 16th Streets. A decade later more than 200 horses and mules pulled 45 cars over 15 miles.

Manure Most Foul

By the 1870s the sight, sound and smell of horse-cars pre-vailed throughout urban America—the sturdily built and some-times elaborately equipped cars, the clip-clop of well-groomed and well-fed horses, and above all the unremitting smell of horse dung. The waste of more than 100,000 horses and mules working more than 6,000 miles of track was overpowering. If each animal emitted just ten pounds per day, a conservative estimate, the total would amount to more than seven million pounds per week—enough to inundate every street and soil every shoe in town, which practically guaranteed that at least some small residue would be carried into every residence and business estab-lishment in citified America.

It was all organic, microbiotic and 100 percent biodegradable, to be sure, but it was still manure, and in the quantities produced definitely a pollutant. Unsightly, unhealthy, foul.

Another health problem—one affecting the horses—struck during the early 1870s. Like the great plagues of the Middle Ages, what contemporaries called the "Great Epizootic" seemed to come from nowhere and appeared unstoppable. It decimated horse populations along the Eastern Seaboard, felling almost 20,000 animals in New York City alone. Actually a type of equine influenza, the scourge gave impetus to fresh quests for alternative power.

Multiple Modes

While horse-cars dominated public transportation through the middle and late 1800s, they never constituted a monopoly. Cable cars and electric trolleys appeared during the century's lat-ter years and omnibuses functioned throughout the entire period, with some hanging on long past their time. On New York City's Fifth Avenue, for example, horse-drawn omnibuses reigned supreme until motorbuses took over in 1905.

So almost from the outset US public transport developed as a congery of multi-modal systems. People at the time probably didn't think about it thus, since the term "multi-modal" wasn't coined until after World War II. But people fully grasped the reality. Numerous cities ran two or more technologies simultaneously.

What isn't so well known today is that US public transport was created by private enterprise and would remain very largely in the private domain for upwards of 100 years. Multi-modal systems sprang from free-market forces, evolving quite naturally from the interplay of consumer demand, production costs and the pursuit of entrepreneurial profits. Because consumers differ widely and because per-rider costs differ too, depending on a welter of factors, businessmen could promote their own profits and economic efficiency as well by offering an array of modes and vehicles on a variety of routes and at various times.

Following earlier patterns, and for much the same reasons, most major metropolitan areas today operate multi-modal systems. Of North America's 25 largest metropolitan areas, 20 offer two or more technologies. Several provide virtually every technology known to mankind. Philadelphia boasts heavy rail, light rail, streetcars, trolley buses and motorbuses. San Francisco runs all the foregoing plus cable cars.

Appealing Conveyance

Cable cars gave a brief respite to some of the horses and mules laboring for the more than 400 companies running street railways. Nor were horses the only beneficiaries: Residents of the cities that opened cable lines enjoyed them, too. And doubly blessed were San Franciscans who enjoyed cable from its inception and who use it still.

Combining concepts from the mining industry with ideas from public transit, Andrew Smith Hallidie, a London-born engineer and wire-rope manufacturer, created what to many aficionados stands as the most appealing conveyance ever built. The story is that Hallidie was motivated by his pity for the poor horses whose bestial jobs looked especially hard and dangerous on the steep hills of San Francisco. Using great ingenuity and $100,000 in capital—a tycoon's ransom back then—he opened a half-mile line up Clay Street hill in 1872.

The line worked by means of an endless steel cable running underground in a protected slot between the tracks. Steam engines at one end of the track, which was later extended for miles, kept the cable moving forward. The driver reaching down below street level with a claw-like device called a "grip" would take hold of the cable when he wanted to go and would release it in order to stop.

San Francisco embraced cable with open arms. And why not? Cable was speedy and clean, with no stable stench, and it afforded a ride both satin smooth and eerily quiet. And according to a newspaper account at the time it even "promoted congeniality among citizens of all classes." And as with both earlier and later means of transit, property owners who had denounced cable's approach rejoiced in the higher property values actually engendered.

Among the 25 cities that would eventually try cable, Chicago and Denver stand out. Chicago built the country's biggest system. At the peak it ran 1,500 cars on 85 track miles.

Cable in Denver

Relative to population Denver did as much and maybe more with cable than Chicago. Denver Tramway Corporation began cable service in December 1888, rather late in cable's history. Constructing its powerhouse at Colfax Avenue and Broadway, the site of today's Civic Center, it deployed routes northwest on 15th Street, east on Colfax and south on Broadway.

A competing firm, Denver City Cable Railway, built its powerhouse at 18th and Lawrence Streets.[2] The powerhouse utilized seven cables, the longest running over six miles out to Gaylord Street and 38th Avenue. This was arguably the nation's longest line. Denver cable at the height of its success accounted for 700 cars on 45 track miles.

As desirable and delightful as cable appeared to the senses, it was also fraught with serious problems. For one, cable proved enormously costly. Powerhouses plus complicated underground paraphernalia boosted capital needs. Difficulties in monitoring and maintaining cables raised operating expenses. Another weakness: As cables lengthened and curves grew increasingly necessary, overall performance became less and less efficient. This limited the scope of service at a time when demand was growing apace with urban geography.

But it was the coming of the electric trolley that led most decisively to cable's relatively quick demise. Electric-powered trolleys would win out over steam-powered cable cars because they ultimately proved more flexible and economical. They could also be extended more readily to the furthermost reaches of the nation's expanding cities and spreading suburbs.

Notes

1. Charles Dickens, *American Notes*, NY; Modern Library, 1996.
2. This original building, a classic Victorian brick, still stands. Now a designated historic structure, it is occupied by the local branch of The Old Spaghetti Factory restaurant chain and includes numerous trolley mementos. One may even sit inside reclaimed trolley cars—albeit with slightly more comfortable seating than they originally offered.

3

TROLLEYS TRIUMPHANT
Frank Sprague's Marvelous Machine

The road to Richmond, Virginia, the site of the first enduringly successful electric streetcar, was strewn with bright ideas that ultimately faltered.

Efforts to propel vehicles by electrical impulse go back to the middle 1800s when Thomas Davenport, a blacksmith living in Vermont, used batteries to operate a miniature car around a circular track. Many inventors over the next several decades would conduct further battery-driven experiments. The upshot? Even the strongest batteries couldn't yield the sustained energy needed to propel bulky vehicles.

So sometime around 1870 creative attention focused on other means of transmitting electrical power. Among the many researchers who worked the issue over the next several decades, here are five who almost climbed to success but who fell just short of providing regular service:

• **Thomas A. Edison**, America's most famous inventor, put together an electric railway during the early 1880s that could go 40 miles per hour, fast enough to scare the pants off anybody daring enough to try it. But for some reason, whether a hidden flaw or perhaps a decision by Edison to concentrate on electric lights, the machine never left his research compound at Menlo Park, New Jersey.

• **Ernest von Siemens** built a short electric railway for the 1879 Industrial Exposition in Berlin. Later he constructed mini-lines for commercial use in Germany and somewhat longer facilities in Northern Ireland. Siemens also founded the firm that eventually became today's giant Siemens A.G.—the company that fabricates electrical components for the light-rail cars Denver currently uses.

• **Leo Daft**, an English immigrant, was responsible for America's first electric railway in regular operation. The year was 1885, the place Baltimore. Because of voltage and short-circuit problems, however, the three-mile line soon shut down and horses replaced electricity. Daft went on from this failure to a long and prosperous career in building cars that would serve all over the country. Some of these employed a device called a "troller" to help convey power to car motors. From this technical lingo, the word "trolley" emerged as a common name for streetcars taking power from overhead wires.

• **Sidney H. Short**, a professor at the University of Denver, opened one of the world's first electric streetcar lines in July 1885. It ran along 15th Street in downtown Denver between Court Place and Larimer Street. Power flowed along a cable conduit at street level and almost immediately people began complaining about shocks received from inadvertently touching both rail and conduit. As one citizen put the matter, "People are dying to ride Professor Short's contraption." The consequence: Electricity was derailed in 1887 and replaced by horses. Later on, after electric streetcars achieved enormous popularity, the University of Denver would be called "Tramway Tech"—not because it sat at the end of a trolley line but because so many students earned their tuition by working as conductors.

• **Charles van Depoele**, born in Belgium, came to America at an early age. Here he established a handy-man business and began tinkering with electric vehicles. After showing his wares at the Toronto Agricultural Fair, he traveled to Montgomery, Alabama, where he had been invited to try his hand at electrifying the Central City Street Railway. Beginning in April 1886 electrification gradually extended so that Montgomery boasted the first citywide trolley system. One problem: Van Depoele put heavy motors on the front platform of comparatively fragile horse vehicles. The results: Cars shimmied and shook, occasionally to the point of disintegration, leaving many observers convinced that electricity could never replace equine power.

Success and Emulation

"Streetcars," "trolleys," "trams," "light-rail vehicles"—all terms are in current vogue and all designate electric-powered cars providing public transport. They may run at street level (at grade), in the air (elevated) or underground (subway). When running at grade they may be in general traffic or in segregated lanes (grade-separated). They can accept power from either a third rail or from overhead wires, but when running at grade in traffic they must use overhead wires for safety's sake.

By whatever name and in whatever configuration, these electric cars first showed the world what they could really do in February 1888 when 31-year-old Frank Julien Sprague picked up the challenge, launching his brainchild in Richmond, Virginia.

The goal rang clear: a public-transport system that could reach reasonable speeds without causing pollution; one offering a comfortable ride while transporting lots of people; one that could run in all weather while affording safety to both passengers and pedestrians. And, finally, something that would bolster rather than diminish property values.

Tough goals, especially with a tight budget, and Sprague

needed all his considerable wizardry to achieve them. What he brought to the task—something his predecessors had not—was formal training in mathematics and science. A recent US Naval Academy graduate, Sprague had undertaken postgraduate work in physics and would later author numerous articles for professional journals. Most of those who preceded him depended pretty much on trial and error and the qualities Mark Twain celebrated in *Connecticut Yankee*.[1] Whether or not the differences in background made for the difference in execution, one thing is certain: Where others failed, Sprague succeeded.

Running at grade and drawing sustenance from overhead wires, Sprague's offering passed every test. It proved financially feasible, neighborhood friendly and technically sound—and it took the transit industry by storm. Within two years after the Richmond inaugural in 1888, electric trolleys by the hundreds were carrying passengers in Cleveland, Minneapolis, Pittsburgh, St. Louis and Tacoma. And before long the hundreds jumped to thousands and the number of systems multiplied 30-fold. Sprague equipped at least half these systems. Most of the others relied on his patents or emulated his planning.

Phenomenal Performance

Never before or since has a new technology catapulted into a commanding position quite as rapidly as electric trolleys. Steamship, automobile and even computer growth appear sluggish by comparison.

In 1890, the first year the federal government took a transit census and two years after Sprague's success in Richmond, electric trolleys accounted for 1,200 miles of track or 15 percent of the total. By 1902 the number had shot up to 25,000 miles or 98 percent of the total—a stratospheric growth rate amounting to almost 30 percent a year for the entire 12 years. A phenomenal performance.

Denver didn't plunge into trolleys with as much exuberance as the rest of the country, the reason being twofold. One, Denver transit companies had only recently invested big money in cable cars. Two, Denver's economy had fallen on desperately hard times. The trouble began in November 1893 when President Grover Cleveland and Congress repealed the Sherman Silver Purchase Act, which guaranteed minimum prices for silver ore, then Colorado's leading industry. The same day silver prices tumbled, silver mines closed down, 11 banks failed in Denver alone, and massive layoffs began hitting construction sites, retail shops and virtually every other business. The economic blast simply leveled Denver, with aftereffects that lingered for years.

Under such severely depressed conditions and given the financial difficulties some of Denver's transport moguls soon encountered, including multiple bankruptcies, it is surprising Denver caught up with the country as quickly as it did. But by the turn of the century Denver boasted a comprehensive streetcar system, with ownership consolidated under the newly formed Denver City Tramway Company.[2]

Cable cars soon disappeared in Denver, as did horse-cars, with one small exception: the Cherrelyn line. Running a short distance south from Orchard Place on Broadway, the line featured horses that would pull a car up the hill and then ride back down standing on a rear platform. What a big kick this gave a generation used to seeing horses do all the heavy work: Dobbin coasting along in leisurely splendor. The spectacle belonged uniquely to Denver and it lasted until 1910, largely as a tourist attraction. (Authentically rebuilt, the Cherrelyn car is now on display at Civic Center in Englewood, Colorado.)

Prosperous Decades

No product or industry can expect to sustain 30 percent annual growth rates forever and only a few can keep up the pace for more than a year or so. Clearly the trolley surge had to slow down. And so it did.

The next quarter century nevertheless would turn out very good for public transport, bringing it prosperity and stability—although the years on other accounts would be full of change and roller-coasting.

The United States in 1925 was very different from the United States in 1900. Fashion, politics, technology—all had undergone fundamental transformations. Demographically, the country had changed too, going from mainly rural to predominately urban. And the national economy, while moving strongly ahead with respect to total output, experienced great volatility. From the end of the Gay '90s to the middle of the Roaring '20s the economy suffered four major traumas. Two were sharp business recessions—the banking panic of 1907-08 and the downturn of 1920-21—both of which plummeted further than anything seen during the post-World War II era. The other two were exceptionally wild swings in general price levels—the inflation of 1914-18, when prices more than doubled in less than four years, and the deflation of 1920-21, when prices dropped some 50 percent.

Decline Begins

Trolleys and public transport weathered the changes and turbulence quite successfully. Not only did they prosper, but they also ingratiated themselves into virtually every aspect of daily life. Standard trolley cars—which were far from look-alikes since they came from many different companies and bore marks of individual craftsmanship—were designed primarily to take people from home to work and back again. But during the salad days specialized vehicles also made the scene. There were party cars for holidays and celebrations, deluxe parlor cars to haul the brass around, cars painted in somber black for funerals, garbage-hauling cars, fire-fighting cars, street-sprinkling cars. There were US Post Office cars arrayed in white and gold. There were sightseeing cars and open cars for balmy-day excursions to parks and picnics. There were even prison cars, legally separated into sections, one for the convicted and another for those awaiting trial.

The year was 1926 and few could imagine life in these United States without electric trolleys. It was just 100 years after Abraham Brower first introduced public transport to American streets, the year trolley trackage reached its apogee of 30,000 miles, and the year daily boarding on all transit climbed to almost 50 million.

It was also the year public transport began to decline. The path down from here wasn't always steep or uniformly straight, and during exceptional interludes like World War II it could veer sharply upward, but for the most part and for the next 50-plus years public transport in America trended mainly downward.

Notes

1. Mark Twain, A *Connecticut Yankee in King Arthur's Court*, NY; Charles L. Webster & Co., [c. 1889].
2. Between 1890 and 1900 more than 25 individual firms provided public-transport services in the Denver area. These were consolidated into two firms: The Denver City Traction Company and The Denver Consolidated Tramway Company. These, in turn, were molded into the Denver City Tramway Company, incorporated 3 March 1899. The new company was led during its early years until 1913 by William Gray Evans, son of Territorial Governor John Evans. It was headed by Howard S. Robinson, a Denver Attorney from 1927-57, and from 1957 to its demise in 1969 by W. A. Alexander, also a Denver attorney.

4

DECLINE AND FALL
OF ELECTRIC TROLLEYS
Not All Change Is Progress

While the decline in overall public transportation seemed bad, the tumble in electric-trolley usage was much worse. Pretty near fatal in fact.

Public transport and electric trolleys—both suffered from the coming of private automobiles and both would be hurt later on by misguided public policies. But electric trolleys confronted yet another problem and confronted it alone: rubber-tired internal-combustion motorbuses. Relations between trolleys and motor-buses started off amicably enough with the original notion being that buses would serve as auxiliaries. They would work sparsely populated areas and feed passengers to heavily traveled trolley routes. Trolleys, with their roomy cars and pleasant rides, represented the mode of choice for mainline service.

Goodbye Old Friends

But as time went by supporting-player buses began nibbling at the wheels of major-player trolleys and in an increasing number of instances the supporting players began to gobble up the principals. During 1933 San Antonio's system became the first big-city outfit morphed into an all-bus situation.

In Colorado, as in most of the country, trolleys vanished first in smaller towns and cities. Boulder, Cripple Creek, Colorado Springs, Grand Junction and Greeley had all lost their lines by the late 1930s. Fort Collins' municipally owned system proved an exception to this general trend, hanging on until 1951. It had by then gained modest celebrity among transit connoisseurs for its spiffy interchange. Three lightweight Birney cars (named for Stone and Webster's chief mechanic) running over three single-track alignments would meet every 20 minutes during peak hours at the corner of Mountain and College Avenues. Here in a flurry of movement the cars swirled in and out and past each other before scooting off in different directions.

Down in Denver, where locally owned Woeber Brothers Carriage Co. produced almost all rolling stock, doomsday came on a prison-gray Saturday, 3 June 1950—just 60 years to the day after Denver Tramway had launched its first successful trolley along Larimer Street. Many Denverites (some would say most) felt sadness and puzzlement at the company's largely unexplained decision to abandon trolleys. Greatly reduced in number from their heyday, the last cars bore posters showing a trolley transfigured with a humanized face and teardrops falling from its headlight eyes, saying "Good-bye Old Friends." Riders debarked with the feeling that this day might someday be regretted. The prophecy proved right on.

Skeletons of Long Departed Lines

What happened in Denver happened across the country. Hundreds upon hundreds of trolley systems fell victim to either drastic curtailment or outright abandonment.

Cities with major rapid-transit systems—such as New York, Boston, Newark, Philadelphia and Cleveland—retained some commitment to electrically propelled public transport. Washington, D.C., San Francisco and Baltimore joined these older efforts with new underground systems of their own. But the vast majority of the nation's cities and towns either ripped up their trolley rails or more likely paved them over with asphalt. Denver is by no means the only town where street repairs routinely reveal the skeletons of long-departed lines. All of which leads some citizens to ask why these lines were abandoned in the first place—and has led still others to note the adage:

Not all change is progress.

Some of these sentiments doubtlessly spring from nostalgia: The "pop" of blue electricity when cars accelerate, cozy windows, yellow lights streaming down to slickened pavement, small boys hitching rides on rear stanchions. Maybe none of these was quite as wonderful as ladies and gentlemen of a certain age are apt to remember. But then trolleys were romanticized even before they died. Almost a century ago, some riders took to them so fondly they collected timetables and dreamed up ways to travel all the way from, say, Boston to Philadelphia on electric cars, using only ingenuity and a pocketful of nickels.

Toonerville and the Gleason Show

But as for the men and women who actually drive the trolleys and motorbuses, they've never been glamorized. Unlike locomotive engineers and airplane pilots, they've not been idolized by small children. Nor have they been lionized by adults.

America's best-known motorman was probably the one-man crew who trundled around on Fontaine Fox's single-track, one-car Toonerville Trolley, a widely syndicated comic strip of the 1920s and '30s. Comedian Jackie Gleason created the country's most famous bus driver when he invented Ralph Kramden, the leading character in *The Honeymooners*, a spectacularly popular TV comedy series of the 1950s. Gleason, whose mother had worked as a ticket agent for the New York City subway during the Great Depression, sported a Transit Workers Union button on the driver's jacket he wore while playing Kramden and reputedly frequented Brooklyn bus barns to gather program material.[1]

By the early 1960s internal-combustion engines had smothered almost every self-propelled electric trolley (some still call them streetcars) in America. Remnants remained in several localities, but mostly would-be passengers began to forget what trolleys were all about—what they looked and sounded like and how it felt to ride them.

Whenever relics did survive, they became affectionately

appreciated. Celebrated internationally as the locale of Tennessee Williams' *Streetcar Named Desire*, which transmogrified into Bus Route #82 in 1948, New Orleans managed to save its six-mile St. Charles Streetcar Line and finished up a major rehabilitation project in 1992. "It's a great transit asset, carrying more than 20,000 passengers a day," said former New Orleans Mayor Sidney Barthelemy, "as well as being an important tourist attraction. We wouldn't dream of changing it."

Radical Replacement

Nationwide patronage statistics reveal how precipitously trolleys plummeted compared to motorbuses:

- In 1926 trolley riders outnumbered those on buses by a ratio of 6 to 1.

- At the outset of America's entry into World War II in 1941 and then on through the war years, the numbers on both modes ran just about the same.

- By 1960 patronage had more than reversed itself, with bus riders outnumbering those on trolleys by a ratio of 15 to 1.

Electric trolleys were born in the USA. They chalked up their first commercial successes in America and they gave Americans a first-class system at a time when public transport in London, Berlin and Tokyo was still mired in horse manure. Trolleys are as indigenous to America as jazz, baseball and abstract expressionism. Why then were trolleys killed off in the United States while they and their latter-day incarnations were viewed throughout most of the world as both winsome and essential?

The superficial answer is that motorbuses are basically superior to electric trolleys and whenever the two go head to head buses naturally win out in a Darwinian struggle for survival.

The alleged superiority arises, the argument goes, because buses can maneuver into and out of traffic, swoop curbside to pick up passengers and move independently of fixed guideways. All of which is true enough but was equally true of omnibuses—the same omnibuses that lost out early on to horse-cars running over fixed guideways. Clearly the foregoing attributes aren't sufficient to make petroleum-powered motorbuses universally superior to trolleys.

What about costs per rider? Were buses cheaper to own and operate? Probably so under some circumstances—as, for example, when operating along lightly traveled routes. But the opposite is true along heavily traveled routes where trolleys can perform for less per ride than buses. What happened during the 1940s and '50s, however, was that buses began replacing trolleys wholesale, whether in the suburbs or central cities and whether they were meagerly or copiously patronized.

Wasteful from a community point of view, this radical replacement seems now to have been terribly overdone. Today, a more balanced outcome—one allowing buses and trolleys to collaborate—would have served both consumer and nation more effectively.

Notes

1. Joshua Freeman, *In Transit*, NY; Oxford University Press, 1989.

5

Fixed Fight

Government Bias and Corporate Conspiracy

Things turned out the way they did because government policies favored buses and because Big Autos and Big Oil, taking advantage of an already weakened opponent, unleashed a series of predatory attacks on trolley systems. The fight between buses and trolleys was . . . well, in a word, "fixed."

According to conventional economic analysis, the less government interferes in competitive markets the more efficient production will be. Companies that make the best products will prevail, and customers can enjoy higher quality at lower prices. In the market where buses and trolleys met, governments intervened early and often.

While treating trolleys as private business, federal, state and local governments viewed rubber-tired motor vehicles as worthy of enormous subsidies. Between 1945 and 1965, more than 90 percent of government expenditures on transportation went into streets, roads and highways with less than 1 percent going for subways and surface trolleys. The consequence was both inevitable and expected: more automobiles and fewer trolleys. The rule here stands virtually inviolate: When you want more of something, you subsidize it.

Underwriting Their Own Demise

Another rule of economic life, equally certain, is when you want less of something, you tax it. Most state-and-local governments followed through by taxing trolleys in decidedly discriminatory ways. Trolley systems were not only obliged to build and maintain their own roadways and pay the interest cost thereon, they were also required to remit significant state and local ad-valorem taxes for the privilege of doing so. Procedures varied from community to community, but the usual approach treated all vehicles, roadbeds, overhead wiring and generating substations as real property. Prevailing valuation standards applied and the legal mill rate charged. The result: Trolleys wound up paying two to four times as much in state-and-local taxes on rider capacity as buses (including the so-called "user" taxes levied on motor fuels).

The problem was very much like the one faced by US railroads in their battle with over-the-road trucks—except that it became even more debilitating. Franchise agreements between trolley systems and municipalities sometimes required systems to pick up as much as half the cost of paving and repaving the streets where they operated. Not only did this requirement mean higher trolley costs, but it also encouraged greater automobile use—which left trolleys in the position of underwriting their own demise, an indignity roughly akin to being forced to cut one's own throat.

Salt Lake City during the late 1920s provides an early illustration of how such arrangements caused the abandonment of rails in favor of rubber tires. Rather than pony up for a large levy to repave a four-mile stretch, the Utah Light and Traction Company simply tore up the affected trackage.

Other discriminations include:

• Franchise agreements often called for trolley companies to clear snow for several feet on either side of their tracks. This work might be the only snow removal on some streets, which encouraged autos to drive down trolley rights-of-way, packing snow and ice into rail flangeways and generally hindering performance.

• When traffic engineers began their love affair with one-way streets during the 1940s and '50s, they determined that trolleys would conform precisely. Refusing to consider even the possibility of contra-flow lanes, they insisted that trolleys either come up with new alignments or shut down. Such demands helped send Denver trolleys to an early grave.

• Municipal officials have long believed that trolleys should foot the bill for all public-purpose amenities along their rights-of-way. And although these attitudes make neither economic nor social sense they persisted into the 1990s.

Conspiracy

The story of how General Motors, helped by Standard Oil and Firestone, moved to wipe out the weakened trolley industry has been told in detail by Bradford C. Snell in his report, *American Ground Transport*, submitted to the US Senate Subcommittee on Antitrust and Monopoly in February 1974.

General Motors concocted a subsidiary called United Cities Motor Transit in mid-1932. "Its sole function," Snell writes, "was to acquire electric streetcar companies, convert them to General Motors motorbus operations and then resell the properties to local concerns which agreed to purchase General Motors bus replacements." The program ceased, however, in 1935 when General Motors was censured by the American Transit Association for its self-serving role as a bus manufacturer, in apparently attempting to motorize Portland's electric streetcar system.

In 1936 General Motors moved on to organize a new and separate corporation called "National City Lines." During the following 14 years, Snell continues, "General Motors, together with Standard Oil of California, Firestone Tire and two other suppliers of bus-related products, contributed more than $9 million to this holding company for the purpose of converting electric transit systems in 16 states to General Motors bus operations. The method of operation was basically the same as that which General Motors employed successfully in its United Cities Motor Transit program: acquisition, motorization, resale . . . By 1949, General Motors had been involved in the replacement of more than 100 electric transit systems in 45 cities . . . In April of that year, a Chicago federal jury convicted General Motors of having criminally conspired with Standard Oil of California, Firestone Tire and others to replace electric transportation with gas- or diesel-powered buses and to monopolize the sale of buses and related products to local transportation companies throughout the country."

The court fined General Motors a grand total of $5,000 for its offense. This was no punishment, not even a symbolic tap on the tush. This was a wink and a smile—and, alas, a get-out-of-jail-free card from the ol' Monopoly game. All it was in truth was an invitation for General Motors to keep on with whatever it was doing. As Snell goes on to say:

Despite its criminal conviction, General Motors continued to acquire and dieselize electric transit properties through September 1955. By then approximately 88 percent of the nation's streetcar network had been eliminated. In 1936 when General Motors organized National City Lines, 40,000 streetcars were operating in the United States; at the end of 1955 only 5,000 remained. In December of that year, General Motors bus chief Roger M. Kyes correctly observed: "The gas motor coach supplanted the interurban system and has for all practical purposes eliminated the trolley."

Angels of Mercy

General Motors offered two intertwined explanations for its behavior. One, the systems it killed were about to die anyway. And, two, who says it's criminal to smash woebegone stragglers?

The first excuse seems disingenuous at best. If trolleys were about to die of their own accord, why did behemoths such as Standard Oil and General Motors need to give them an over-the-brink push? They didn't, of course. Not unless Standard Oil and General Motors were acting as angels of mercy from some Industrial Right-to-Die ideology. Standard Oil and General Motors . . . angels of mercy? A quaint idea, isn't it?

As to the denial of criminal guilt, this skirts the issue. The heart of the matter is whether poor public policies together with private influence can lay waste to a major industry and thereby impede American access to serviceable mass transit. To this question, the answer is plainly yes—although it would be exceedingly difficult to say how responsibility ought to be divided up. Nobody knows exactly how to apportion blame between government policies and private aggression.

Presidents' Conference Committee Cars

Squeezed by government bias on one side and by big business attacks on the other, the presidents of 25 US trolley companies coalesced to create the Electric Railway Presidents' Conference Committee. Their purpose was to design a thoroughly modern vehicle—one that would halt passenger losses.

After several years of research conducted at Ann Arbor, Michigan, under the direction of Professor C.F. Hirshfeld, the new vehicles—called Presidents' Conference Committee (PCC) cars—reached Brooklyn neighborhoods during late 1935. Their reception ranged from enthusiastic to ecstatic. One writer called them the "most notable achievement in the history of public transportation." Citizens from all boroughs came for a sample ride and many started taking the long way home just for the joy of swooshing along on what *The New York Times* hailed as the "harbinger of a new era."

PCC cars delivered markedly better rides than their predecessors, with the solid steel wheels of old giving way to "sandwich" wheels composed of layered steel and rubber. Improved motors seemed scarcely audible. Car brakes screeched no longer and boxy car bodies turned sleek and streamlined as did almost everything from radios to toasters to gasoline pumps during the Art-Deco 1930s.

Although the Great Contraction of 1929-33 dealt the national economy a smashing blow and would deliver another with the recession of 1937-38, the new cars attracted numerous buyers. More than a thousand were purchased and put into service by the time Japan attacked Pearl Harbor on 7 December 1941. Not one, however, found its way to Colorado.[1]

During the ensuing war years PCC output continued while private automobile production shut down. War-production officials decided that new trolleys, unlike new automobiles, were essential to the war effort—and they scrambled to get every available vehicle onto rails and into the vital job of moving defense workers. It was during this period that trolley boardings reached an all-time daily peak and that they accounted for their largest total-trip percentage.

PCC output and technical improvements continued into the early postwar period. Indeed, some of the more notable advances came after the war ended—as, for example, the use of all-electric equipment to replace air compressors and air brakes. For a few halcyon years, it appeared streetcar companies might reasonably aspire to a prominent place in a national system of multi-modal transport. The United States, after all, led the world in trolley production and technology. A high-potential infrastructure of rails and electrical-transmission facilities already existed nationwide. And consumers preferred trolleys over buses by whopping margins, according to about every item of statistical and anecdotal evidence available on the subject. [2]

Destroying an Industry

But widespread multi-modal systems with trolleys plying the heavily traveled routes were not to be. San Francisco placed a final order in 1951, receiving 25 cars from the St. Louis Car Company during the next few years. It was the last domestic order for PCC cars.

Two conclusions should be highlighted:

• Although consumers would have liked and would have bought more trolley service, their preferences did not prevail. The failure stemmed primarily from government bias and corporate intrigue.

• When trolley producers lost their domestic market, they forfeited their ability to maintain a smaller but substantial market overseas.

Whereas firms such as J.G. Brill of Philadelphia and the St. Louis Car Company once exported finished cars and essential components around the world, they were now reduced to shipping a few secondhand derelicts. Whereas these firms, along with General Electric and Westinghouse, once established American-managed trolley plants in France, Great Britain and Holland, they now sold their patents and licenses to foreign investors.

For upwards of 50 years the United States had dominated world trolley markets. No more. America lost a major industry to overseas competitors—the first such loss during the years following World War II. So when it came time in 1991 for Denver's Regional Transportation District (RTD) to buy light-rail cars for its 5.3-mile Metro Area Connection (MAC), there wasn't a single US producer who had the machines, the workers or the know-how to manufacture the necessary components. While these vehicles were assembled in Sacramento, California—and shoehorned into federal government Buy-America guidelines—the fact remains that most sophisticated elements came from Germany.

Not Inevitable
Did things have to turn out the way they did? Did the death of the US trolley industry result from an unremitting dialectical or technological process? The answer is no.

With regard to government, it is clear that spending and taxing policies did not have to be pro-automobile and anti-trolley. They could have been neutral; they could have been pro-trolley and anti-automobile. Either way, our urban landscape would look quite different than it does today.

Apropos General Motors, one can say with certainty that the world's largest and most powerful industrial concern, which accurately describes General Motors at the time of the events recounted here, did not need to smash its trolley rivals in order to survive or prosper. Maybe the better question is whether General Motors' officials would have behaved differently had they known then what they know now. Has the rueful distress of watching their own company's share of world markets drop, and then drop some more, altered their views about right and wrong?

Possibly yes . . . but probably no. Normative views don't seem to change very much or very often. But maybe this time around a remembrance of things past could help moderate the persistent anti-trolley attitudes found throughout the Highway Users Federation, a powerful lobbying group that Alfred P. Sloan, General Motors' longtime chairman and CEO, created some 50 years ago. A creation still going strong today.

Handicapped in Financial Markets

The vast majority of American public-transport companies were locally owned and operated. And although they cut a noticeably wide swath on the hometown scene, they were by many relevant standards decidedly "small." Along with small businesses of all kinds, they lacked access to national capital markets.

What this "thin" access means is that small businesses carry handicaps compared to large businesses when pursuing long-term funds. Sometimes, even when willing to pay above-market interest rates, small businesses still can't clear all the financial hurdles in their path; still can't borrow the funds needed to expand and improve performance. Such was the widespread situation throughout the middle 1930s and early '40s (and to some degree today). Many local lenders and investors, still spooked by the financial collapse of 1929-33, squeezed hard on small business firms, including small trolley companies.

Although small themselves, some trolley companies overcame their financial handicaps by virtue of being owned by much larger organizations, usually public-utility holding companies. This relationship enabled them to tap national capital markets and helped them raise the money they needed to buy modern rolling stock. These arrangements, sad to say, would not survive the vagaries of the New Deal.

Public Utilities Holding Act

Early New Dealers such as Rexford Tugwell and Adolph Berle argued that the best way to fight the Depression was through economic concentration tempered by the central control of production and prices. But the demise of the National Recovery Administration (NRA) by Supreme Court decree signaled a new direction.

Buttressed by the legal theories of Supreme Court Justice Louis Brandeis, together with the aggregate-demand theories of British economist John Maynard Keynes, the New Deal moved toward reestablishing a competitive economy. A key was the breakup of utility holding companies. At the center of this approach stood the *Public Utilities Holding Company Act of 1935*.

Introduced in the US House of Representatives by Texas' Sam Rayburn (D) and in the Senate by Montana's Burton K. Wheeler (D), the holding company law required electric-power companies to divest themselves of their transit subsidiaries. This requirement deprived subsidiaries of crucial financial backing at a time when they had virtually no alternatives. Intended to strengthen competition and small business, the law actually punished trolley companies and lent a helping hand to Big Autos and Big Oil.

Notes

1. Numerous citizens, together with *The Denver Post*, urged Denver Tramway to give PCC cars a trial run. Tramway officials refused, however, saying "No good purpose would be served by bringing in equipment there was no intention of using." *Denver Tramway*, S.C. Griffith, Electric Railroad Association, NYC, Dec., 1961.

2. Consumer surveys aren't available to demonstrate the point because public opinion polling back then was positively primitive. The *Literary Digest* poll, highly respected in its day, predicted that Alf Landon would overwhelm Franklin Roosevelt in the 1936 presidential election. The Gallup poll predicted a Tom Dewey victory over Harry Truman in 1948.

6

INDUSTRY LEADERS

Public Transport Never Rationalized

Perhaps all the roadblocks—government bias, big-business attacks, capital-market snafus—wouldn't have counted so heavily had public transport been led by the kind of men Matthew Josephson depicted in *The Robber Barons* (1934)[1] or that later writers more favorably inclined toward National Football League-type capitalism call "Captains of Industry."

But no such leaders appeared to do for public transport what John D. Rockefeller had done for oil, J.P.Morgan for steel, Walter Durand for automobiles or Bill Gates for personal computer operating programs. Public transport would never be "rationalized."

Transit leaders seemed talented enough. And a varied lot they certainly were. One leader, distantly related to the European house of Rothchilds, inherited wealth and lofty social position. Another grew up poor and left home at an early age to seek his fortune as a hard-rock miner. Another leader inspired a major novelist to base an admiring trilogy on his career. And still another found himself sharply attacked by a broadly acclaimed author who ignored his accomplishments while sensationalizing his legal entanglements.

But for first one contingency and then a second and a third and so on, none of these individuals nor the myriad others who controlled the business end of public transport could surmount the economic and governmental impediments facing them. The industry's business leadership never chalked up anything like the successes scored by its engineers and mechanics.

Some of the diversity in leadership, and some of the reasons why obstacles confronting the industry weren't wholly overcome, suggest themselves in the following vignettes:

• *Samuel Insul* (born 1859, died 1938). Born in London into a family of religious dissenters, Insul immigrated to America as Thomas Edison's personal secretary. He became president of the Chicago Edison Company at a time when the electrical industry was small and scattered, and from this base took off on an extraordinary ascent to wealth and power—controlling in time companies generating a full 10 percent of all US electricity. And having entered what was then called the "traction" business as a way to sell more electricity, he would dominate public transport in and around Chicago, including both elevated and surface lines.

Then came the crash. In a matter of months Insul not only lost his wealth and position but became a national symbol of evil, a stand-in for all those whom Franklin D. Roosevelt excoriated as "malefactors of great wealth." Novelist John Dos Passos in *The Big Money* called him the "Power Superpower," who suffered from "the illusion that the money was all his."[2] Charged with mail fraud and other offenses, Insul saw himself brought to trial as representative of an era, not as an individual. "If two men had walked down Fifth Avenue a year ago," he told a guard in May 1934, "and one of them had a pint of whiskey in his pocket and the other had a hundred dollars in gold coin, the one with the whiskey would have been called a criminal, and the other with the gold an honest citizen. If these two men had slept for a year and again walked down Fifth Avenue, the man with the whiskey would be called an honest citizen and the one with the gold coin a criminal."[3] What had happened to the legal code during the interval was the repeal of Prohibition and passage of the "gold clause" outlawing private possession of monetary gold. What had happened to American business practice was the Great Depression.

The courts finally found Insul not guilty of criminal charges, and put into historical perspective the courts seem right. Certainly, in light of what would come later— corporate kleptocracies such as Enron, Tyco, Qwest, Adelphia, WorldCom, Arthur Andersen and so many more—what Insul did seems innocent enough. Even so, his transit properties fell off into receivership. His cars continued to run into the 1980s, well past their 50th birthday, but the opportunity for Insul to rationalize public transport had long since passed.

• ***Winfield Scott Stratton*** (born 1848, died 1902). An obscure carpenter from Indiana who hit it rich in Colorado's Cripple Creek gold bonanza, Stratton bought the Colorado Springs Interurban Railway in 1900 and promptly pumped $3 million into modernization, a sizable sum back when gold sold for $21 an ounce. Called the "Midas of the Rockies," Stratton planned to build electric lines all over Teller and El Paso counties so that his fellow citizens might commune with the "grand in nature."[4]

His plans never came to pass, but what he actually did struck many as more commendable. A man whom neighbors believed equally given to whiskey and kindness, Stratton became the first corporation owner in America to take out group life insurance for his employees. He also stood among the first to finance a plan whereby his workers could buy their own homes. More than three-quarters of his many employees availed themselves of the opportunity before Stratton's death.

• *August Belmont* (born 1859, died 1924). His father was immensely rich, his mother, Caroline Slidell Perry, a famous beauty—and one of America's early aristocracy. It was her uncle, Captain Oliver Perry, who after an American victory over British naval forces during the War of 1812 sent the stirring message, "We have met the enemy and they are ours." Belmont attended Phillips Exeter Academy and graduated from Harvard. The day after his father died, he took over the family banking firm and excised the "Jr." from his name. Like his father before him, Belmont became a significant player in the Democratic Party—a relationship that led to his appointment by New York City Mayor Hugh Grant to a committee studying underground transit. The committee's proposals came to nothing, as had numerous others over the preceding quarter century. A decade later, however, when yet another subway plan seemed near failure because of funding shortages, Belmont rode to the rescue.[5]

Unique at the time and a faint foreshadowing of today's "privatization," the proposal called for the city to supply the money to build a subway that it would own while private companies leased and operated the lines. Belmont formed two companies. One bankrolled construction-contractor J.B. McDonald. The other operated the Interborough Rapid Transit (IRT). This was Belmont's shining hour as a financier, taking on a monumentally expensive project that most bankers argued would surely fail. He retained an active interest in IRT's affairs until his death, even building an elegantly appointed car named the "Mineola" to use while traveling around town.

At the same time, Belmont showed no interest in expanding beyond New York City. Always an avid sportsman he devoted his later life to thoroughbred racing, with Man O' War being just one of his great horses. The Belmont Stakes, the second contest in racing's famous

Triple Crown, is named after him. His contributions to public transport are largely forgotten.

• *Harry E. Huntington* (born 1850, died 1927). Scion of land and railroad magnates, Huntington acquired a financially weak trolley company in Los Angeles with the intention of putting together a far-reaching and up-to-date transit system, comprising both trolleys for use within the city and electric interurbans operating between cities. He succeeded beyond all expectations until locking horns with H.E. Harriman's Southern Pacific Railroad.

Using its superior political and financial clout, the Southern Pacific stopped Huntington's advance—who soon lost interest in public transport and turned his energies to building a world-famous museum. The city property was ultimately sold to General Motors' insidious National City Lines (see Chapter 5) which as expected scuttled all trolleys in favor of buses. The Southern Pacific Railroad absorbed the interurban part of the empire, calling it the "Pacific Electric" and developing it into the nation's premier interurban system. What locals called the "Big Red Cars" traveled at one time over 1,000 track miles. At the end of World War II, the system began encountering increasing problems, including statewide electrical shortages. But it was the Southern Pacific's decision during the early 1960s to stop all passenger service that sounded the death knell for what had once been a heavily patronized network.[6]

Believing that freeways would eliminate traffic congestion, a majority of the populace stood by without protest as their once-splendid transit system fell apart. (The 1988 movie *Who Framed Roger Rabbit* engagingly depicts the funny but sad public attitude toward The Big Red Cars versus Automobile Freeways.)

- **Charles Tyson Yerkes** (born 1837, died 1905). American novelist Theodore Dreiser chose Yerkes as the model for protagonist "Frank Cowperwood" in his trilogy *The Financier, The Titan* and *The Stoic*. Dreiser viewed Yerkes as a superman who "looked life in the face," a man whose many personal transgressions deserved forgiveness because of his spectacular rise in a world where the author believed only the fittest survive. Others saw Yerkes as a corrupt financial plunger who acquired and then tossed aside a long succession of badly treated mistresses. Still others thought of him, more simply, as a hard-driving entrepreneur who almost—but not quite—succeeded in unifying traction systems in Philadelphia, Chicago and London.[7]

Whichever view hits closest to the mark, Yerkes left neither heirs nor dedicated followers. His ferociously flamboyant efforts to consolidate the trolley business disappeared with his passing.

- **James H. McGraw** (born 1860, died 1948). He was one among several businessmen who neither owned nor managed any part of the trolley industry but whose ancillary role led to prominence in other fields. McGraw began publishing *Electric Railway Journal* in 1908 as a medium for selling capital equipment to trolley operators. This was the first in the incredibly long and still growing list of magazines produced by the McGraw-Hill Company, one of the largest publishers in the country today.

Later on, as the trolley business declined, the fortunes of *Electric Railway Journal* declined along with it—a downward spiral that McGraw-Hill executives found themselves reluctant to discuss with the aging founder. They needn't have hesitated. When finally given the unhappy news, McGraw asked but one question: "Is it making any money?" When told it wasn't, he responded without pausing a sentimental second: "Then kill it."

Counterfactual

Is it plausible to ask "What if?" To ask "What would have happened if public transport had been rationalized?" Really and truly rationalized—to the degree that newly consolated firms could reap what economists call "economics of scale?" Including scientific management, access to national capital markets and research and development?

The questions are counterfactual, of course, but they aren't irreversibly sappy—not like "What would General Robert E. Lee have done at Gettysburg if General George E. Pickett's Virginians had an atomic bomb?" After all, consolidation could have happened and probably would have happened under just slightly altered circumstances.

With the birth of the Presidents' Conference Committee car, industry leaders demonstrated quite amply their ability to introduce new technologies—and to sell technical advances to consumers in attractive ways (see Chapter 5). Where leaders fell short was in accumulating the managerial and political prowess needed to forestall government discrimination and big-business ambush.

It would be enormously irresponsible to deny that automobiles were destined to assume major roles in urban mobility or to gainsay that trolleys were fated to lose large hunks of their market share. Such changes were undeniably in the cards—especially in the wake of post-World War II prosperity and suburbanization.

On the other hand, it is entirely reasonable to argue that in a more equitable environment other scenarios could have spun out differently. Domestic trolley service needn't have died, and US trolley production needn't have migrated to foreign shores. The major conclusion: Neither "creative destruction," a term *grâce a* Austrian economist Joseph Schumpeter, nor a natural withering away provides the complete story of how American trolleys lost their dominance and almost fell from sight. Vigorous and quite personal blows to the midsection played an important role as well.

Even a marginally effective trolley system would seem preferable to no trolleys at all. Something beats nothing every time.

Notes

1. Matthew Josephson, *Robber Barons; The Great American Capitalists*, NY; Harcourt, Brace & Co., 1934.
2. John Dos Passos, *The Big Money*, NY; Harcourt Brace & Co., 1936.
3. Forest McDonald, *Insul*, Chicago; University of Chicago Press, 1962.
4. Frank Waters, *Midas of the Rockies*, Denver; University of Denver Press, 1949.
5. David Black, *King of Fifth Avenue: The Fortunes of August Belmont*, NY; Deal Press, 1981.
6. Thomas S. Shank, *From Horse-Car to Red Car*, Virginia Beach; The Donning Company, 1991.
7. Theodore Dreiser, *The Financier*, Cleveland; The World Publishing Co., 1940.

7
GOVERNMENT-OPERATED PUBLIC TRANSPORT
Denver's Regional Transportation District

Rescued by the Great Depression that left many Americans too impoverished to buy suburban houses and new automobiles and later by World War II that stopped the production of these things, the US public-transport business entered the postwar years with unrealistic expectations. Basking in wartime importance and profitability, many transit leaders seemed to think they had a hammerlock on an absolute necessity. They were mistaken. Although few seemed to realize it, time was already running out for privately owned public transport.

Peace and prosperity, the *summum bonum* for most Americans, weren't just unkind to transport; they bludgeoned it into bankruptcy. Transport's capital and operating costs kept rising while its erstwhile patrons kept acquiring new automobiles and moving to the suburbs and exurbs—places where privately owned public transport wasn't prepared to follow.[1] All of which raised the question of whether service should either be shut down or taken over and operated by government.

Much the same question had been asked before, long before at the turn of the 20th century. Reasons for asking back then may seem farfetched today but were deemed serious enough at the time to persuade popular periodicals like the *Atlantic Monthly* and learned journals like *The American Economic Review* to explore the question in depth. The issue then revolved around whether transport's market position might be too formidable— whether it might constitute a natural monopoly requiring government ownership to prevent price-gouging.

What a comedown! By mid-century the question concerned market weakness. Specifically the question had become whether public transport should be allowed to fade away or should be rescued and continued as governmental enterprise.

It is very odd to remember that intellectuals once considered public transport a "natural" monopoly. It was nothing of the sort, of course, and many economists today doubt the generic existence of such creatures. Even at its zenith, transport operated as a fragmented "technical" monopoly with a short life expectancy. Now the industry seemed quite simply too debilitated to sustain itself. More than just winding down, it had begun to look like a burnt-out case rushing pell-mell to extinction.

Given the choice between government-controlled transport or none at all, most US communities opted for government ownership. Transport presented itself as too important to be left for dead. Consequently, the next several decades—the '50s, '60s and early '70s—were transitional. Hundreds of properties changed proprietors. North, South, East and West, private firms devolved into government agencies. The transformation is now complete. Nowhere in the United States can one find a privately owned, self-supporting public-transport company.

Private Tramway Becomes Government RTD

Changes in Denver actually didn't occur until fairly late during the process. Not until mid-1969 did Denver Tramway Company officials advise then-Mayor Bill McNichols that because of continuing losses they would soon be forced to close. The mayor, together with City Council, moved quickly toward a buyout, and city voters approved the acquisition in November 1970. Mayor McNichols spoke out in discontent about the $4.5 million price, contending it was unfairly padded with large sums for Tramway's now quite worthless franchises. But the deal was nonetheless consummated in April 1970, and Denver city government proceeded to cinch up its belt and raise the sums needed to pay the asking price.[2]

Earlier, recognizing the desirability of a regional system, Colorado's General Assembly put together the Regional Transportation District (RTD) to cover the urbanized portions of six counties.[3] RTD became a legal entity on 1 July 1969 with sufficient funding for it to act as a planning agency. Introduced in the Senate by John Bermingham (R) and in the House by Ted Bryant (R), the initial bill also contained provisions for holding a district-wide tax referendum providing construction and operating monies.

As political efforts are disposed to do, the ensuing tax campaign enticed voters with various hard-to-deliver promises. The most effective: In exchange for a district-wide 0.5 percent general sales tax, RTD would provide a multi-modal public-transport system—a system including local buses, regional buses, express buses and 93 miles of small electric-powered vehicles called "Personal Rapid Transit" (PRT). Many political analysts contended that PRT alone gave the campaign the pizzazz it needed to succeed. The tax referendum was held at a special election in September 1973. The public approved by a vote of 57 to 43 percent.

Appointed Board of Directors

Thus did RTD take over public transport in the six-county metropolitan region. While saddled with a host of promises to deliver, it was likewise blessed with the financial wherewithal to start acquiring 13 small transit companies, to order a relatively large fleet of new buses and to undertake serious work on rail-based rapid transit.

How did RTD do? The answer: not well. Not well at all considering the fulsome promises and hopeful expectations.

Governance headed the problem list. The legislature created a 21-member board of directors and bestowed upon it total responsibility for all RTD actions. Denver's mayor appointed ten members; county commissioners from the surrounding area appointed nine; the appointees themselves picked two.[4] The board in turn was authorized to elect a chairman from within its membership and to hire a full-time manager who would be charged with running the agency's day-to-day affairs.

An early recruit to the general manager (GM) job was John D. Simpson, a West Point graduate and stout advocate of by-the-book regimentation. Establishing a strictly hierarchical chain of command, Simpson positioned himself as king of the hill and packed almost everybody else off to sit in Coors' Field Rockpile, an escape-proof bleachers from which no one can exit either into the grandstands or onto the greensward. The board of directors accepted Simpson's dictatorial ways with a weak-kneed compliance that quickly became second nature.

Three Deficiencies

Much of the population saw the board and its top managers as failing them with a resounding thud. The following deficiencies jumped out:

> • **No rail.** To woo votes for the impending September 1973 sales-tax election, RTD held a hurriedly assembled exhibit at downtown Denver's Currigan Hall. Here it showed off the neat little four-passenger cars everyone would soon enjoy—if the majority voted to underwrite them of course. Well, a substantial majority (57 percent) of the half-million voters cast their ballots the right way, but nobody got to travel around in the swell little cars. The reason: No rails were ever installed and no cars ever procured.
>
> The failure here—RTD's inability to keep a clear and straightforward promise, together with its unforgiving collection of the taxes morally tethered to that promise—did not sit well with the community at large. The deadly combination would create a climate of distrust, rancor and even scorn-a culture that soon became entrenched. Excuses were proffered naturally, but few if any were swallowed—either whole or in part.

• *Lousy bus service.* Thoroughly exasperated by RTD's failure to demonstrate even a rudimentary sense of fidelity, riders drew little consolation from highly touted improvements to bus service—largely because nobody could discover any. Renamed "The Ride" by RTD's public relations experts, the overall system still didn't work like even a wayward bus system should. Despite huge boosts in total spending and employees, service looked and felt no better than before. The average bus was usually dirty and frequently late and sometimes didn't show up at all (called "missed runs"). Drivers were often grumpy, as were passengers, and it took forever to rouse anybody in the customer information office. Worse, wheelchair lifts designed to help disabled patrons malfunctioned in weird and threatening ways, putting distraught users into physical danger and leaving shocked onlookers in dismay. These ordeals—flesh and blood disasters actually—dragged on month after month, year after year.

But RTD saved its most withering fusillade for a single day, the Tuesday following Labor Day weekend of 1978. Riders woke on this sunny morning to find their accustomed bus stops missing. Some stops had moved just across the way; others a few blocks up the street; and still others appeared to have vanished in billows of blue-black diesel smoke.

What on earth had happened? The board had accepted and put into effect something its staff called the "Grid System"—a doctrine so addled in concept and so faulty in execution that it conjures a picture of logistical vandalism, something deliberately dumb and destructive. In concept it decreed that all buses follow straight lines, *straight lines only.* No more turning corners, no more maneuvering to popular destinations, no more squiggling through tightly packed neighborhoods. What about passengers who neither lived nor wanted to travel along straight routes? Why, the answer came back, "Let them transfer"—an answer about as poorly thought out as Mademoiselle Antoinette's "Let them eat cake." As anybody in the business understands, transfers are the *bete noir* of successful public transport. A sure-fire way to discourage riders. In execution the grid wrought changes in virtually every bus route and bus stop within the entire district—all within a single day. This was an operational disgrace—something also guaranteed to slash ridership.[5]

• *Sleaze.* Adding insult to injury, the appointed board overlaid all these very urgent and thorny problems with a patina of sleaze. It rented private jet aircraft to fly itself around in high-season style. It co-mingled purchases of private vehicles with RTD fleet purchases. It took to violating Colorado's open-records and sunshine statutes blatantly and continuously.

It hired private detectives to probe for dirt in sexual relations between board and staff members. (The gumshoes uncovered plenty that looked awfully tacky but nothing that appeared truly transgressive.) From the outside, what with the voluminous newspaper stories and film-noir gossip, the whole affair looked like a case of spending public monies in order to gratify a voyeuristic propensity on the part of a few insiders. A government subsidy for peeking into other people's windows.

God's Servant

Were it possible to single out any one event as laying the groundwork for the appointed board's ultimate demise, that dubious honor belongs to the Grid System. After the grid, the die seemed solidly cast. Popular pressure for reform never wavered. But equally important perhaps was attitude: The board majority would neither listen seriously to complaints, nor act to address them.

Like British King Charles II, the board simply could not get a proper view of itself. "I am God's servant," thundered the king, "not the people's slave."[6] So, too, the imperious appointed board. With the board majority smugly believing no one could run RTD as well as itself, while much of the public angrily believed no one could do any worse, a political showdown loomed on the horizon. Absolute self-confidence versus total disdain. The major question, although it wasn't clear at the time: Will reform in RTD governance proceed through a legislative referendum or through a public initiative?

Of the alternative roads to a popular plebiscite—public initiative or legislative referendum—the referendum appeared the easiest (appeared so on the surface at any rate). For one thing, more than a few state senators and representatives had grown weary of RTD, had become rankled by the tiresome flow of bad press and fed up with fielding constituent complaints—complaints about events and insults that individual legislators couldn't do anything to correct anyway. Further, not all that many "ayes" were needed to put a referendum on the ballot—only a simple majority. Just 33 out of a 65 total in the House; 18 of 35 in the Senate.

Too Controversial

Not everybody took favorably to the notion, however. The mere idea provoked negative outcries from silk-hat banking and real-estate interests, who lost no time in conveying their agitation to Colorado's legislative leadership. These political leaders in response moved to escape the heat through the use of a time-tested snow job—more specifically, through creation of an ad hoc joint legislative committee designed to look as if it could supply RTD with direction and oversight (Senate Joint Resolution 12, 1979). It couldn't. Toothless and lacking both factual knowledge and solid conviction, the oversight committee did absolutely nothing to relieve the situation, nothing to quiet the roar for reform.

So during the next legislative session (1980) a referendum bill came forward that seemed very likely to pass, thereby bringing the question to a head at the ballot box.[7] But something funny happened on the way to final passage. The bill ran up against an impenetrable roadblock in the House Transportation Committee. Acting within his legal prerogatives but with a sophomoric cynicism toward public transport, Chairman William F. Hilsmier (R) decided he would not bring the bill to a committee vote, which effectively struck it down before first breath. No debate before full House or Senate. No final up or down. RIP.[8]

When asked why, Representative Hilsmier gave one of the more risible answers in legislative history. "The issue," he opined, "is too controversial to be discussed." The issue of whether RTD should be governed by an appointed or elected board is taboo? It's too charged with irrational emotion to bring before 100 elected adults who have just hashed and rehashed abortion, gun control, gay rights?

Amusing? Some thought so. Others thought too clever by half. But mainly the entire affair struck observers as pathetic.

But on one important point most statehouse observers agreed: Chairman Hilsmier had been "gotten to." By whom? By the "establishment"—a word that suggests semantic cop-out, but that in this instance pretty well denotes the sundry groups involved, including personages from the elitist ends of finance, politics and law.[9] The whole affair constituted a paradigm of special interests blocking General Assembly action. A popular and politically backed reform could not pass—could not even receive a hearing—owing to interest machinations. So what could come next? Either start the postmortems or go with a public initiative.

Cheers for Initiative Process
Every once in a while, a political invention comes along that really works—one that cuts the pants to fit the cloth. Such a device is the initiative.

Celebratory assessments of the initiative are no longer as fashionable as they once were. A product of the Progressive Era dating from 1889—the year Jane Adams opened Chicago's Hull House—to 1921—the year Warren G. Harding became president—the initiative has come under recent attack. In recommending it to the citizenry and the 1911 special session of the Colorado General Assembly, Governor John Franklin Shafroth (D) said the initiative process "would produce a purifying and beneficial effect upon every legislative act," and curb "special interests and selfish motives." Now, 90 years later, *Washington Post* columnist David E. Broder denounces it as "a departure from constitutional checks and balances" and as "a subversion of democracy."[10] Historians writing between these poles, when they treat the topic at all, usually kiss it off with either faint praise or quick dismissal.

All of which makes it important to note: Without the initiative process Metro Denver would still suffer rotten bus service and would still limp along without light rail. The cheers heard here for the initiative stem directly from a public-sector job well done. Outcomes do count.

Brave Little Band

Not that mounting a grass-roots campaign resembles in any way launching a financially productive dot-com. How could it when the biggest job in an initiative campaign—collecting voter signatures—is closer to picking cotton or scraping paint than it is to anything liberating or stimulating? What's more, "grass-roots" is an alternative way of saying "broke"—which means that all a genuine grass-roots campaign can offer for the slogging job of knocking on doors or scudding around shopping centers in search of signatures is an opportunity to evangelize and contribute to the body politic. No wonder the vast majority of people—including true believers—do very little in the way of hustling signatures. Most sensible people stay away in droves—sensible people seeking fame and fortune or just a fair day's wage for a fair day's work.

Adding to the built-in predicament Colorado courts sharply tilted the playing field. Because RTD had been created by state legislation, the courts decreed that initiatives dealing with RTD must be decided by the state as a whole—rather than by the geographical area in which the agency operates. This ruling more than doubled the signatures needed to secure a ballot position. Moreover, it bumped the number of counties participating in the election itself from six to 65—the vast majority of which could be fairly said to care less about either RTD or public transport. Had the question been handled through a legislative referendum, the six-county RTD district would have comprised the base.

Great pluck coupled with a little bit of luck—it took both of these to surmount the challenge. A brave little band of some ten persons supplied the pluck, garnering 95 percent of the more than 75,000 required signatures.[11] The luck came toward the end of the signature-collection period when it looked as if the goal might not be realized within the allotted three months.

Then out of the blue came the Denver Art Museum with a serendipitous exhibit devoted to Jim Henson's Muppets. So popular were the Muppets at the time, their committed fans queued up in slow-moving lines three and four blocks long. These queues offered petition circulators a fruitful target, yielding enough valid signers to push the initiative over the top, with a day or so and a handful of names to spare. Take a bow, Kermit. You, too, Miss Piggy.

Elected Board Assumes Command

The rough old road to the ballot segued into tranquillity. The election campaign itself came off relatively free of disputatious charges and countercharges. Proponents hadn't the money to raise a hullabaloo. Opponents believed they could win by playing possum, especially because they assumed that outside the metropolitan area most voters, knowing next to nothing about the issue, would naturally tend to say no.

Just one underhanded incident made headlines. When the

appointed board accused initiative carriers of forging petition signatures and hired handwriting experts to prove the allegation (at public expense naturally) the daily papers played the story prominently. Coverage faded when adversaries backed off with shame-faced acknowledgment that they could find nothing amiss. From a political perspective, the false allegation came across as foolish. The misuse of public money to pursue the charge seemed positively harebrained.

The *Rocky Mountain News* favored an elected board. *The Denver Post* opposed. Out-of-district voters, as opponents fore-saw, leaned against but district voters went heavily in favor. The total statewide count in the November 1980 election mirrored that in the September 1973 sales-tax election: 57 percent yes, 43 percent no. Because of the timing, however, an elected board would not take command until two years later on 1 January 1983.[12]

Reaching Out to Disabled

A momentous upheaval had occurred—no arguing about that. But would the big change result in public betterment? Many citizens remained more than a little skeptical.

Part of the "yes" vote was based on hope but another part rose from pent-up anger—from a fervent desire to throw the rascals out. Could vengeance lead to lasting improvement? Denver's disabled community, led by Wade Blank who had long before established an advocacy group for the disabled called "Atlantis," had an early opportunity to find out.[13]

The occasion: Many months of Atlantis protests—petitions, picketing, disruptions, arrests—had left the appointed board adamantly unmoved. It simply would not include wheelchair lifts in its recent order for 89 new buses. The elected board ended the ruckus at its very first meeting. With deepened sensibilities and a quickly executed policy reversal, the elected directors added lifts to the new bus order. Additionally they agreed to start retrofitting the existing fleet.

Giving RTD a second chance, these steps transformed searing hostility into lasting friendship, quite fortunately for everyone concerned. The skies always brighten just a little when providers and patrons manage to settle crucial differences without coming to blows or getting themselves tossed into jail.

But outside RTD the battle over accessibility raged on, with Colorado Governor Dick Lamm leading the forces of reaction. Beginning his political career as a moderate pro-choice, slow-population-growth Democrat, Lamm had started during his later terms to lecture the elderly on their "duty to die" and to inveigh against spending public monies on teaching disabled children "to roll over." Given a prominent platform by the American Public Transit Association (APTA)[14] at its annual meeting held in Denver that year, Lamm sternly suggested that accessibility on all public-transport buses would amount to $600 per trip. "If we can't say no to a system that costs $600 per trip," he piously intoned, "we don't deserve to continue as a great nation."

Lamm's laugh-out-loud figures were wrong by a magnitude of 50 to 100. His tone came across as that of a sanctimonious scold. Vitriol kept the pot stirred but it failed to stop RTD's farsighted policies. By the time Congress passed the Americans with Disabilities Act in 1990, RTD had raced miles ahead of most US transit agencies in complying with federal standards.

Repairing a Broken System

It is no exaggeration to say that when the elected board took over RTD, the agency was comporting itself unprofessionally in bus operations and unrealistically in rapid-transit planning. It looked to many users about as impotent with large taxpayer subsidies in its coffers as Denver Tramway Company had looked without them. The principal way to tell the two organizations apart: At RTD no one seemed to care. The cavalier mantra "take it or leave it" prevailed throughout.

The lack of professionalism in bus operations showed itself very plainly in ridership statistics. Boardings fell, both as a percent of all trips, (including auto, bicycles, etc.) and in absolute numbers, throughout the appointed board's ten-year tenure.[15] During its last year in office the numbers dropped to the lowest levels ever. An impressively awful record.

Had RTD been a private business and suffered similar carnage, it would without doubt have slipped into a Sargasso sea of insolvency. As a free-standing government with guaranteed sales-tax revenues, it drifted on financially while treading water operationally.

All in all, the first reasonable priority was to re-establish the bus system as a living, breathing entity. This the elected board took steps toward doing by firing then-GM Kim Kimball whose primary merit lay with light-rail planning and salesmanship. He was replaced by Ed Colby who stood as a "first" at RTD—the first general manager genuinely committed to running a consumer-oriented bus system, and the first with a record showing he was savvy enough to put a convenient and dependable operation on metropolitan streets. Colby also knew most procedural details and liked working the daily treadmill as well as big-ticket expansion issues.

Along with the crucial revitalization of attitudes and personnel, the elected board also introduced a raft of programmed correctives. These honed in on bus-rider beefs. Among the programs: elimination of missed runs; 30-minute headways; customer relations training for all drivers; new schedules; revamped signage; and speeded-up wheelchair-lift repair.

From Last to First in a Decade

Even so, board members discovered that improvements came neither quickly nor easily. It had been a bureaucratic party going down, but it generated a massive public headache climbing back. Several years of sweat and struggle passed before rider confidence and boardings began to recover. But the ruins were ultimately repaired and professional standards gradually approached. RTD won APTA's prestigious award as North America's number one public-transport system in 1992.

Not bad for an agency that ten years earlier had ranked by general consensus as North America's worst. Pretty good, actually.

Notes

1. The largest road-building program in US history, the Federal-Aid Highway Act of 1956, encouraged residents to move out of Denver proper and into suburbs and exurbs. Justified by President Dwight D. Eisenhower on the grounds that a vastly improved interstate highway system was needed for the swift evacuation of urban residents in the event of nuclear war, the program wound up serving more mundane ends. For example, it promoted automobiles and discouraged public transport.

2. Mayor McNichols saw the issue quite clearly. The price was wildly excessive for a few rickety buses and a near-obsolete repair facility.

3. All or parts of Adams, Arapahoe, Boulder, Jefferson, Denver and Douglas counties.

4. The following were members of the original appointed RTD Board of Directors: Leo F. Sullivan (Denver), John Fleming Kelly (Denver), Richard C. Thomas (Denver), James M. Bowers (Boulder), Perry Eberhart (Adams), Elwood M. Kullgren (Denver), John R. Crowley (Arapahoe), Jean R. Arthur (Arapahoe), Robert F. Clement (Jefferson), Ann K. Beckwold (Boulder), Herbert Cook (Denver), Maynard Bellerive (Adams), John Harper (Jefferson), Samuel R. Freeman (Denver), Donald B. Robertson (Denver), Earl Howe (Denver), Leo Rodriguez (Denver), H.C. Kimbrough (Douglas), Wendall T. Liggins (Denver).

5. Absurd, baffling, late-summer madness. If this were a novel, the foregoing account of the Grid System would have to be dropped on the grounds that it lacked fictional credibility. The story is nonetheless entirely true.

6. Stephen Coote, *Royal Survivor; A Life of Charles II*, NY; St. Martins Press, 2000.

7. House Bill 1134, Representative Jack McCroskey, Prime House Sponsor.

8. Coincidentally, Representative Hilsmier owned and operated an agency selling auto insurance in Longmont, Colorado.

9. Among the political elite: House Speaker Beverly Bledsoe from Limon, where public transport was not an issue; House Majority

Leader Carl Gustafson who held contracts with Denver Mayor McNichols as city bond advisor and sometimes underwriting principal. McNichols was especially keen to keep the RTD appointed board and his power to appoint ten RTD directors.

10. David S. Broder, *Democracy Derailed: Initiative Campaigns and the Power of Money*, NY, Harcourt, 2000. A strangely lopsided and grouchy book by a widely intelligent and highly acclaimed journalist. Broder essentially ignores wide swaths of geography and many examples of genuinely good grass-roots initiative campaigns. I am wholly mystified. Colorado's last three governors supported initiatives in the furtherance of their overall programs. Richard Lamm's (1975-86) initiatives concerned tax reform; Roy Romer's (1987-1999) concerned education; Bill Owen's (2000-) covered gun control.

11. Among the stalwarts: Ethlyn Christensen, Mike Henry, Miller Hudson, Jerry Kopel, Jack McCroskey, Betty Neale, Jim Perrin, Jack Phinney.

12. The newly elected directors taking office on 1 January 1983 were: Jack McCroskey (District A), Tom Bastien, (District B), Larry Perry (District C), Ann Walton (District D), Byron Johnson (District E), Mary Duty (District F), Dick Karam (District G), J. Bear Baker (District H), Bill Womack (District I), Kathy Williams (District J), Casey Hayes (District K), Don Feland (District L), William Johnson (District M), Bill Rourke (District N), Roger Cracraft (District O).

13. Not disabled himself, Wade Blank possessed an implacable concern for social justice and served as an outstanding spokesman for the disabled. He died 15 February 1993 while trying to save his son, Lincoln, from drowning. His work with public transport is commemorated in Denver's Civic Center Station.

14. The major public transit trade organization with about 1,100 members, including transport systems, product and service providers, and departments of transportation. Its products include publicity, publications and meetings. It also lobbies for public-transport funding at the federal level. During fiscal 1999, RTD paid the association about $75,000 in total fees and charges.

15. Boarding, trips, passengers, etc., are tricky and often misunderstood (sometimes deliberately) measures of public transport. They are used interchangeably, which they are not. Boarding constitutes the industry's basic measurement. A "boarding" is defined as a technical term that counts each time a passenger enters a transit vehicle—bus, light rail, access-a-ride or mall shuttle. A passenger traveling from point A to point B without transferring vehicles chalks up one boarding. But if the trip requires a transfer, the journey is counted as two boardings. Consequently, if a passenger taking a bus to light rail, then rail to downtown and then uses the mall shuttle, it's counted as three boardings. A round trip such as the latter counts as six boardings. Thus, one common-sense "trip" can equal three boardings—or six boardings per round trip.

8

TROLLEYS REDUX

Turning Rapid-Transit Talk into Light-Rail Action

Time: *Winter 1988*
Place: *Board Office, Regional Transportation District*
Problem: *Light Rail. All Talk, No Action*

Denverites had been talking about building rapid transit for longer than most people could remember—and the talk actually went back beyond living memory, back a hundred years and more to the late 1800s when University of Denver Professor Sidney Short built one of the world's first electric streetcars along 15th Street between Court Place and Larimer Street.

So what was the public legacy from all the decades of big talk and rancorous argument? What had the community gained? Anything?

The cul-de-sac answer during the winter of 1988: two public referenda, an aborted state agency, a governor's roundtable, a long string of private and public commissions—plus interminable planning, traveling and speech-making. Altogether, not counting indirect community spending, outlays here mounted to well over $100 million. An appalling sum. Especially since there were still no rails and no trains—and no realistic strategy for acquiring any.

Defeat by Default and Election

The first referendum came in 1973 when voters were asked to approve a 0.5 percent sales tax in return for expanded bus service *and* personal rapid transit. Voters said yes, but the rapid-transit part of the promise collapsed when the federal government refused to contribute financial assistance. RTD then shelved the idea, complaining that by itself it couldn't possibly come up with the requisite money.

The second referendum took place in 1980, the same year the proposal for an elected-board passed. RTD then asked voters to approve a 0.75 percentage-point boost to its existing sales tax, with the proceeds earmarked for construction of a 77-mile light-rail system. Voters rebuffed the request 54 to 46 percent.

Shouldn't these results have rung down the curtain on light rail? A lot of citizens certainly thought so. Some even bought into a rhetorical sneer they would never tire of repeating. "What part of no," they needled rail's well-wishers, "don't you understand?"

But other citizens envisioned other possibilities. To these people the prevailing antipathy aimed more at management than at light rail. Lackluster performances by both board and bureaucracy should be held responsible for the failure to build tracks and trains. Light-rail champions could therefore take heart. If RTD could just be cajoled (or hammered) into cleaning up its louche behavior, another contest on yet another day would yield a victory.

This was one opinion. A more radical view held that RTD would never reform itself and consequently ought to be replaced. A tight coalition—including the influential Greater Denver Chamber of Commerce,[1] the Denver Technological Center and Governor Roy Romer (D)—became especially keen on replacing RTD. So the coalition decided to act decisively. It would pressure the General Assembly into starting a brand new government. Giving in to these forces, the Assembly created the Transit Construction Authority (TCA).

Raised Up and Cast Down

Newly spawned governmental units promise both change and continuity—a different way of ordering things naturally, but also a permanent presence. Markets sometimes crash, businesses come and go, congressional incumbents occasionally stumble.

But governments and governmental agencies? In the United States these are as timeless as Thanksgiving Day and the Pledge of Allegiance. Once in place they stay. Attesting to this are the *National Tea Testing Board* (established 1795) still dunking crumpets in Washington, D.C., and *Colorado's Sunset Review* (established 1980) which still hasn't vanquished even one of the dozen and more state licensing boards its sponsors had hoped to plow under. If statuary were erected for defunct government programs rather than departed heroes, Washington would look more like a strictly commercial venue than a capital city.

Highly unusual in its vulnerability, the TCA constituted a welcome change from the general rule. Born in the Colorado legislature May 1987, it died in the same place August 1989, after 27 months of useless but high-maintenance existence. Legislators bought the TCA idea in the first place largely because they had been promised the new agency could build rapid transit using private monies, augmented by small infusions from federal sources.

But the TCA actually received taxing authority at the very outset when empowered to impose both property and employment taxes along the Southeast Corridor, running from downtown Denver to the Technological Center, a major employment center on the city-suburban border connected to downtown by Interstate 25. But when the agency started collecting revenues, it stirred up unexpected resistance—the sort of demonstrative naysaying that looked as if it might have escaped from the 1960s.

Wearing fake Indian headdresses, smoking funny cigarettes and toting symbols of the Boston Tea Party, tax protesters literally hooted TCA off the public stage. The legislature could not resist this tax rebellion, which combined the political clout of both large and small businesses with an irrepressible media circus. When the end finally came only Howard Gelt, sometime leader of the Colorado Democratic Party, showed signs of bereavement. As the last standing executive at TCA, Gelt mourned alone.

Failed Takeovers

Made of sterner stuff, Governor Romer neither mourned nor attended the funeral. He was busy scouting alternative ways of taking over light rail. (Nobody demonstrated much interest in usurping RTD's control of the bus system. Politically and economically ambitious folks considered buses profitless and more than a little déclassé.)

The governor failed in the end but not for want of trying. First, he convened a 60-member Transportation Roundtable and charged it with formulating new ways of structuring public-transport's governance and finance. The Roundtable, after a five-month study, sent recommendations to Colorado's General Assembly, which in turn created a nine-member Metropolitan Transportation Development Commission (MTDC). The details of MTDC's suggestions were scrambled and then souffléd as they sloshed around the legislative frying pan, but the key priority remained unchanged: Strip RTD of the powers and revenues needed to build rapid transit, then turn these tools over to somebody else.

Deadly serious about the matter, Governor Romer advised a group of RTD directors, *fortissimo*, that if they "didn't stay out of his way, he would roll over and crush them."[2] He tabbed attorney Tom Strickland, chairman of the Colorado Transportation Commission and US senatorial aspirant, to spearhead his agenda, and he enlisted a horde of mercenaries (lobbyists) to help spread the word. He also picked up explicit backing from several RTD directors, including Roger Cracraft (District O) and Henry Solano (District D), contributing to the erroneous impression that he was dealing a friendly game. No way was this the case. Visceral hostility reigned throughout.

The governor very nearly pulled it all off nonetheless. After passing the House, his measure fell just one vote shy of the 18 needed to carry the Senate. A midnight roll call on the last day of the 1991 legislative session told the tale. Potent and persistent attempts to wipe out RTD had flopped.[3]

Tax Windfall

Meanwhile, the board majority, happy to see the attempted coup d' etat finally fall through, redoubled its efforts to deliver rider-friendly, multi-modal public transport. Having brought back during the middle 1980s a semblance of professionalism to bus service and restored a smidgen of customer confidence, the board had turned its attention toward redeeming RTD's original pledge to build rail-based rapid transit—although a humongous question at the time was why anybody with any brains would bother with Denver light rail. After so many years of promising and reneging, proposals and counter proposals, failed elections and political mud-wrestling, the whole notion had come to look and sound completely phony. More like a "Humbug" from Ebenezer Scrooge than an affirmative "God bless us everyone" by Tiny Tim.

Nevertheless, with a great deal of hard thinking and a little sharp figuring, some board members began to discern fresh ways of swinging light rail without a tax election. The genesis of the new perception? Credit should go to the Colorado Supreme Court, which without much prior notice deposited a tax windfall into grateful board member arms. The Court ruled that RTD should start collecting so-called "use taxes."[4] Properly understood and boldly exploited, this good fortune could give light rail a mighty leg up.

Three-Legged Stool

To borrow a celebrated metaphor from Edmund Burke's *Reflections on the French Revolution*, a successful rail startup resembles a sturdy three-legged stool.[5] Each leg must be firmly in the right position for a proper stool or viable project. Misplace or lose any of the three, the stool cannot stand and the startup cannot function as intended. They will crash.

The three legs: Funding, Technology and Alignment. While work can proceed (and usually does) on all three simultaneously, each leg propounds its own questions. Each question requires its own answers.

Original Corridor Funding

If local governments had all the money they wanted, funding wouldn't pose a problem. Of course not. Nor would it if local governments could do as the federal government does and monetize their debts. But these are fantasies rather than realities, which leaves local governments facing a simple truth: They must raise in one way or another whatever they spend. As with ordinary businesses and everyday families, they cannot create money.

The federal government can. This unique power may go to the bottom of why federal politicians generally seem less humble and not so down-to-earth as their state-and-local counterparts. It's certainly the reason state-and-local governments act somewhat more prudently in their spending and why they should attend very carefully to costs. Unfortunately, putting rail together is not just expensive—it's excruciatingly so, running from $25-50 million per mile.[6]

With its use-tax ruling the Colorado Supreme Court gave RTD a relatively small boost in cash flow, the increase being estimated at the time to reach around $7-9 million annually. This sum wasn't nearly enough by itself to jump-start rail—not even enough to lay a single mile.

Much of what was needed here was the understanding that although additions to pots of money cannot be significantly multiplied, additions to cash flows most certainly can be—with the value of the multiple (or lever) depending primarily on credit worthiness and market interest rates. Given RTD's AA credit rating and low interest rates generally, the $7-9 million addition to annual cash flow could be leveraged to raise upwards of $100 million through the issue of 20-year tax exempt bonds. This sum amounted to just about what it would take to underwrite five miles or so.

Two conclusions need underscoring here. First, the Colorado Supreme Court did nothing out of the ordinary: It merely corrected an unjustifiable discrepancy among governments. The Court said that so-called "use-taxes" are part and parcel of general sales taxes, and further that RTD is entitled—as state-and-local govern-ments almost universally are—to collect levies on items bought outside but used inside its jurisdiction.[7] Second, if these funds had not been spent building rail, they would have likely disappeared into RTD's bureaucratic maw, generating dead-end studies and administrative redundancies, with little or no improvement in customer service.

High marks should go to the elected board for its courageous and creative decision. Fortitude as well as foresight was needed to take a stab at something so strikingly different. By no means the only tax windfall RTD or other local governments had ever enjoyed, this windfall may have been the very first to fuel construction of a major public project. An important local-government innovation.

Original Corridor Technology

With $100 million and a bit more to spend on new plant and equipment, RTD felt obliged to settle rather quickly on the tech-nology it wanted. Many alternatives appeared available—options that should be mulled over at the very least. Among these were personal rapid transit, diesel locomotives, subways, elevated lines, mono-rail, magnetic levitation.

But for one reason or another most novel alternatives dropped from contention early on. Only surface light rail fit all the criteria: safe and non-polluting, reasonably priced to build and operate (as such things go), time tested, attractive to riders and acceptable to the community as a whole.

Discontent surfaced during public meetings about RTD selecting a 19th century technology, which some critics viewed as hopelessly out of date. A valid gripe in part, perhaps, but one that held equally true for automobiles. Nickolaus Otto introduced an automobile powered by a four-stroke internal-combustion engine in 1876, Gottlieb Daimler the same in 1885. The first sustainable electrical trolley system didn't appear until 1888 in Richmond, Virginia. The truth is that both light rail and motorbuses descend

from antique lineage—a fact that is in any case irrelevant to selection of the appropriate mode for a particular time and place.

More to the point was the face-off between "Cutting Edge"
and "Tried-and-True." Cutting Edge, although brimming with
dazzle and millennial excitement, struck most board members as
both too costly and too chancy. Not only were financial
resources acutely limited, the non-technical and marketing risks
inherent in launching a new transport system seemed daunting
enough in and of themselves. Would people like it? How many
could be coaxed into actually using it? Nobody knew the
answers—not for sure. What the board recognized full well: If the
project were to fulfill its role as the linchpin for future opportunities, there could be no faltering during the debut—no cost
overruns, no construction delays, no operational breakdowns, no
mechanical aberrations of any kind.

In the end the board went with thoroughly tested surface
light rail, determined not to invent anything and insofar as possible to buy absolutely nothing that couldn't be taken directly off
the shelf. The results? Construction of the original line came in
on schedule and under budget. Operational breakdowns have
been few and far between.[8] About 50 percent more people than
originally expected board it. And if there are those who feel
unfairly deprived because the ride isn't sufficiently 21st century,
they keep their complaints to themselves.

Selecting Original Alignment

So by leveraging a relatively small use-tax windfall to the
maximum, RTD could eke out roughly five light-rail miles.
Nowhere near the 93 miles envisioned at the beginning in 1973,
these five miles nonetheless represented a start toward redeeming
the promise: *To build rapid transit within the existing 0.6 percent
sales-tax rate.*[9] (A promise that by this time many citizens considered basically bogus.)

The remaining question: Where to put it? A tough issue
made more difficult by the need to start with a very short line

inside an immense district. Sprawling over six counties and 2,300 square miles—many of them sparsely populated—RTD encompasses an enormous area by comparative standards. It's geographically three times as large as systems in either Phoenix or Orange County; twice as big as those serving Atlanta and Portland; one-and-a-half times the size of those in Washington, D.C., and New York City. And yet Metro Denver's three-million population base is less than the base in these other cities.

Perhaps sheer geographical size had more than a little to do with the delays and difficulties RTD encountered in starting rail. It can be intimidating to take the first step along what everyone suspects will be an agonizingly long and uncertain journey.

The stakes were huge. Not that a $100 million mistake would break RTD—it wouldn't, not even if the sleek light-rail cars transmogrified into lumbering white elephants. The biggest hurt would lie in choosing a site where light rail would fail to demonstrate its full potential. While literally hundreds of places could be found where a five-mile demonstration line would wind up looking foolish, there were only a precious few where it could show itself as a star-spangled winner.

Too Dinky

Amid the worries and doubts clouding selection, just one certainty lit the public-process firmament. No matter which location the board finally chose, many citizens would pounce on that choice as wrongheaded.

How could it be otherwise? Dozens of neighborhood activists pushed to be among the first beneficiaries. Even more clung to the motto: "Not In My Back Yard," aka NIMBY. Some of the most powerful people among the area's commercial and political establishment disdained and opposed building a line they considered shamefully dinky.

In the latter group stood the politically macho and high-profile Richard C.D. Fleming, president of the Denver Metro Chamber of Commerce. Fleming dearly loved to portray himself as a transit

visionary and trailblazer. But like many members of his organization he had fallen in thrall to the fallacious theory that rail
requires building every which way at once. This idea left him
aridly unsympathetic to RTD's incremental approach. For
Fleming and his misguided confreres, building light rail had
frozen into an inflexible "either or"—either build everything at
once or build nothing whatsoever.[10]

Sample and Centerpiece

When an action appears ridiculous on the surface, it's often
just that, ridiculous. But on rare occasions something superficially
silly turns out on further examination to be certifiably sensible.
Such was the case with RTD's decision to anchor its demonstration line in the middle of downtown Denver. This was the only
place a five-mile line could serve in the short run as a sample and
over the long haul as a centerpiece.

> • *Sample.* For folks who couldn't remember streetcars
> and hadn't tried light rail in another setting, the need for
> a working demonstration appeared self-evident. Some
> citizens feared rail would sound boombox loud; others
> believed it would hightail it along built-up roadbeds
> made of white rock; still others took all positive claims for
> rail with a heap of salt. A prominently located and easily
> accessible demonstration line would help dispel these
> misgivings.

> • *Centerpiece.* But if citizens welcomed rail with open
> arms, as appeared likely, finding it an attractive and
> effective way of promoting mobility, then the Central
> Corridor (called the Metro Area Connection or MAC at
> the time) could extend into other corridors. It would act
> as the beginning link for every corridor—the centerpiece
> of an overall light-rail system. (Illustration I on next page).

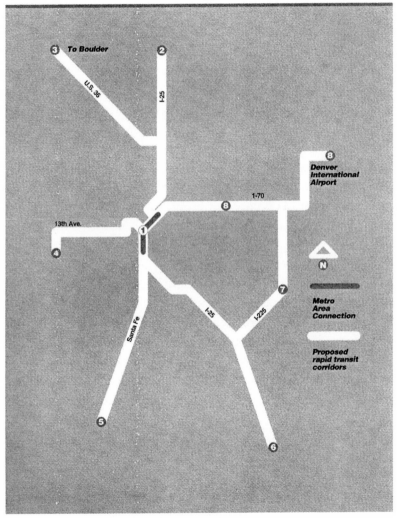

Illustration I

Source: RTD Board of Directors

Northeast Versus South

The decision to use downtown Denver as the starting point opened the conceptual possibility of moving out from the center in myriad directions. Fortunately these possibilities foundered in actuality—"fortunately" because solving a mega-selection puzzle could have stymied the project for years, maybe forever. In reality, owing to the mix of terrain and demographics, the line could proceed along only two routes: northeast toward Stapleton Airport (which was also the general path toward soon-to-open Denver International Airport) or south toward the quickly grow-ing southern suburbs, including the Denver Technological Center, Littleton and several other parts of Arapahoe and Douglas counties.

Of the two, for manifold reasons, the Northeast Corridor laid claim to being the number one option. First and foremost the five-to six-mile stretch between downtown and Stapleton fit within the limits on length and was therefore financially doable. Centrally located and easy to find, it would attract folks from all over to look and ride and decide for themselves whether they approved. It connected two activity centers and it would . . . well, without rhapsodizing, it would have made an exemplary venue for a demonstration project.

Except it was also the place where a dormant territorial-imperative emerged from its slumber to become a red-toothed, sharp-clawed NIMBY.

Not In My Backyard

This NIMBY just about wrecked the metaphor of the three-legged stool. With two legs securely attached—technology and financing—the alignment leg should have slipped easily into place.[11] It didn't. The alignment question generated instead a hundred and more neighborhood meetings—gatherings where citizens bombarded RTD with objections that couldn't be fully overcome. Among the saddest ironies of the racially-charged pol-itics that dominated the situation: While some members of the

African-American community believed the project was intended quite deliberately to damage their neighborhood, an even bigger crowd of white residents from other neighborhoods saw the project as an under-the-table payoff to African-American politicians.

Neither of these cavils was true. No smoke and certainly no fire rose from either accusation. (What there was of course was 300 years of slavery plus another hundred of sharecropping, lynching and Jim Crow.) Thankfully, neither side constituted anything like a solid phalanx. Amid the continuing controversy, RTD Director Glenda Lyle, the board's only African-American director, led an all-out battle for light-rail service within Denver's traditionally African-American neighborhoods. Ably assisting her were Lawrence Lewis and Gloria Holliday, two widely known and well-respected African-American residents of the affected neighborhoods.[12]

What the matter boiled down to was a sharp split among those living in the affected area which included the neighborhoods of Five Points and Park Hill. On one side of the fence, possibly the majority side, stood those who thought light rail would constitute a boon for one and all. On the other side, certainly the most vociferous side, stood those who contended it would envelope their homes in a smoky miasma of awfulness. Some argued further that light rail would sunder community solidarity by creating good and bad sides of the tracks.

Nor was this all. The most emotionally resonant argument came from State Representative Wilma Webb[13] who held that a rail line down Martin Luther King Jr. Boulevard would desecrate the memory of that great and fearless man.[14]

On the verge of finally starting light rail but with the real possibility of stumbling to a premature halt, the RTD board met on the evening of 25 September 1990 before an overflow audience of more than 250. A "yes" vote by the board would allow light rail to leap forward. A "no" vote would play out as déja-vu all over again—worse really, it would set back the clock on light rail until voters found it within themselves to boost taxes, which from the look of things might not happen until an entirely new generation came of age.

Meeting minutes portray an evenly divided crowd, with 16 speakers favorably disposed and 16 opposed. This written picture is deceptive. Bringing in the camera on the gathering reveals all too many pulled faces and wagging heads, while the sound system droned mainly dissenting murmurs.

The East Denver Ministerial Alliance brought speakers for the opposition. Among them: Reverends Dr. Paul Martin, Acen Phillips, Langston Boyd, Jr. and Bonnie Perry. The Community Advisory Committee offered several speakers in favor: Frank Sullivan, Lawrence Lewis, Yvonne Heather and Marcella Jackson.

With all said and done and despite a mainly confrontational audience, the board passed *unanimously* Resolution No. 8, Series of 1990, calling for construction of a five-mile light-rail line from downtown Denver to Stapleton Airport.[15] Protracted maneuvering down a road strewn with political potholes lay ahead as did a batch of alignment booby traps. But despite the difficulties to come, this night stands as the ignition point. Denver light rail was truly on its way.

Cutting the Baby in Half

Ready and able and actually raring to go, the board nonetheless hesitated before a worrisome ethical question. Should RTD force rail through neighborhoods where so many residents appeared dead set against it? In an earlier America (just 30 to 40 years ago), the question wouldn't have created waves. Whole neighborhoods and even small towns were routinely razed to make room for highways. In order to complete the Cross-Bronx Expressway during the mid-1950s New York's famed bureaucrat Robert Moses used the state's condemnation powers to rip apart a solid mile of small apartments, ruthlessly destroying thousands of family homes. Just a few blocks away there ran a parallel route requiring virtually no demolition.

Heaven forbid anyone undertake anything so unfeeling in 1990. The RTD board certainly had no intention of indulging in such loutish behavior. Bending over backwards, even though it contemplated no condemnations, the board felt obliged to explain to all objectors why light rail down the wide median of Martin Luther King Jr. Boulevard wouldn't create disfigurement, either social or environmental. To this end, the board set off on a marathon of neighborhood meetings designed to explore from all possible angles how light rail might fit in. Several dozen neighborhood activists ultimately traveled to Vancouver, Portland and Sacramento to see for themselves rail in action.

All to no avail. Minds didn't change. Wounded feelings didn't heal. Jagged-edge nightmares about an intrusive flapdoodle as screechy as the Chicago El didn't go away.

Serving Basic Purposes

All this left the board severely conflicted. Although positively obsessed with starting rail, the board decided it would be morally wrong to force the issue against deeply entrenched neighborhood feelings. In a more pragmatic vein, residential support seemed essential for long-term success.

The way out? Cut the baby in half. Thus it came to pass that the original five-mile line shrank to 1.7 miles. RTD kept the part from downtown to the heart of the Five Points neighborhood, terminating at 30th and Downing. It axed the part continuing through Park Hill and on to Stapleton Airport. One newspaper columnist gleefully called the truncated proposal the "Amazing Shrinking Rail Line" (see Illustration II on the following page). Other commentators used even less imagination in advertising the board's embarrassment.

But the plan for the line served its basic purpose of sample and centerpiece at least until further particulars could be worked out (see Chapter 11). It also allowed a predominantly minority neighborhood to enjoy top-quality transport service into downtown.

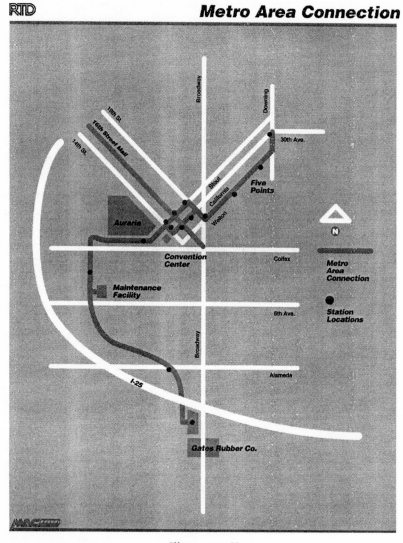

Illustration II

Source: RTD Board of Directors

Notes

1. The Greater Denver Chamber of Commerce changed its name to the "Denver Metro Chamber of Commerce" in the late 1990s. The latter name will be used through the balance of this chronicle.
2. A little aggravating, no doubt, but nothing unusual here. Just an everyday part of Governer Romer's leather-jacket, slipping-around type charm.
3. The favorable outcome here was owing in large part to the stalwart efforts of professional lobbyists John Fisher and Bill McClain.
4. A use tax is generally defined as a tax on all tangible personal property used or consumed in the course of doing business that was not otherwise subject to sales tax in the business' home jurisdiction. This usually means a product purchased in another jurisdiction where no sales tax was applied at the time of purchase. The details of this definition and the specific items covered (or exempted) will vary somewhat from one jurisdiction to another.
5. Edmund Burke, *Reflections on the French Revolution*, NY; J.M. Dent & Sons, 1910.
6. There are tradeoffs, however. While rail's capital costs run much higher than those for buses, per-rider operating costs can amount to much less. For example: RTD generated the marginal costs for building a 3.4 mile extension to the MAC with savings realized by cutting about 500 daily bus trips along the same route. One issue: Capital costs necessarily occur long before operational savings, raising the central financial issue of how to bring savers and investors together.
7. There is no problem with double taxation. Taxing jurisdictions routinely forgive sales levies on materials delivered outside their areas.
8. Compare and contrast with Denver's 1992 decision to invest in a cutting-edge baggage carrier for Denver International Airport (DIA). The decision delayed opening 14 months and dropped $500 million in public funds down a deep dark hole. The carrier still does not work. Very few observers think it ever will.

9. The original rate was 0.5 percent but the state reduced the sales tax base by removing groceries in 1982, which reduced revenues by an estimated 20 percent. The legislature sought to make up the loss in base by adding 0.1percentage point to the rate. Rate x base = revenue.

10. Despite long-standing support for tax increases designed to build rapid transit, Denver's organized business community for the most part opposed building a demonstration light-rail line *sans* tax increases. For example, prominent members of the puissant Downtown Partnership held repeated meetings to ridicule the idea and jibe at its advocates. Among those sponsoring such meetings: Harry Lewis, investment banker; Diana Boulter, Partnership Executive Director.

11. "Corridors" differ from "alignments" in specificity. Corridors are generally thought of as several miles wide. Alignments specify precise geographic location, such as exact streets and street numbers—in other words alignments indicate just whose house will be affected.

12. Five Points is the historical commercial center of Denver's African-American Community. The name of the neighborhood comes from the five-points intersection where 26th Avenue, 27th Street and Washington Street meet at Welton Street. The only thing Denver's Five Points has in common with New York City's Five Points is the name. Denver's neighborhood was created by racial segregation, New York City's by successive waves of immigration—Irish, Italian, Chinese. For a story of Denver's neighborhood, see: Laura M. Mauck, *Five Points Neighborhood of Denver*, Arcadia, Chicago: 2001. For New York's see: Tyler Anbinder, *Five Points*, Plume, New York City 2002.

13. Representative Webb had succeeded her husband, Wellington Webb, now mayor of Denver, as the state representative for about half the area through which the Northeast Corridor must run. In the Colorado legislature, they had sequentially led the long-term and ultimately successful efforts to establish Colorado's Martin Luther King Jr. state holiday.

14. This assertion was not susceptible to empirical refutation. Since the technical arguments could generally be defined either way depending on one's perspective, about all that proponents

could do was note Reverand King's early and long association with public transport. It was Rosa Parks' refusal to give up her seat on a public transport bus that triggered the 381 day Montgomery, Alabama bus boycott (1955-56). Reverand King, a newcomer to Montgomery and pastor of the Dexter Avenue Baptist Church, helped put together the movement that led to the reversal of segregation laws on public transport—one of the earliest issues in the broad-based civil rights revolution nation-wide.

15. Board members voting yes: Bill Womack District (I); Glenda Lyle (B); Bernard Zimmer (G); Helen Steele (M); Roger Cracraft (0); Dan Gray (H); Jack McCroskey (A); Stephen Millard (N); Kevin Sampson (J); Henry Solano (C); Cameron Winder (E); Robert June (K); Absent: Michael Garcia (D); William Gagnon (H).

9

ALL OR NOTHING AT ALL
How Hate and Love Delayed Denver Light Rail

Light rail is either a waste or a salvation; it should go nowhere or everywhere; it should never be built or should be built all at once. These are the emotional extremes that kept Denver's public transport in the tangled woods of stalemate for more than 30 years. Hate and love combined in ways that rendered the sunlit middle-ground uninhabitable.

Light rail is a technology—a conglomeration of coaches and electric motors, wheels and rails, overhead wires and pantographs that link the moving vehicle to its power sources. It is hard—really very hard—to understand why these assemblages excite such outsized passions.

But they undeniably do—as do the automobiles with which they have a great deal in common. Both autos and light rail are costly, both depend on government subsidies and both seem destined to play essential roles in urban mobility during the 21st century. So why can't autos and light rail get along?

No-Fault Autos and Rail

The answer: They can and do. It's the irrational haters and lovers who keep everyday citizens in the dark about the natural affinity between the two.

Consider the case of the haters. After killing off Denver's last electric trolley some half-century ago—a folly that many senior residents remember with a mixture of anger and sadness—they collaborated with tarmac-mad bureaucrats in covering up all visible trackage. Like the vandals of ancient Antioch who toppled the Imperial Forum, they despoiled their enemies both practically and symbolically. And they joined forces ever after with anybody anywhere who would help inveigh against city-street railways.

On the other side of the bipolar divide—the smother-love side—one finds urban reconstuctionists and environmental evangelists, who as often as not come across as true believers. Nor do these folks stand alone. When light rail comes up for grabs, they are supported politically and financially by special-interest business groups such as the Denver Metro Chamber of Commerce—and also by a thundering herd of investment bankers, plus the passing parade of consultants, developers and contractors. These well-heeled suitors usually seem more interested in government dollars than public transport. Naturally. But mostly no one troubles to distinguish between the two.

Sensible Middle Not Told

So it went. In one corner were the asphalt aficionados who would immolate light rail in a funeral pyre. In the opposite corner were the environmental true believers and their friends of convenience who would schmooze it to death. Together the haters and lovers put together an unbeatable team. The haters served up an unshakable negative vote of roughly 20 percent. The lovers with their untamable appetites could be counted on to turn off another 30 to 35 percent. Added together the negatives come to more than half.

As a partial consequence of all this, many people living within the six-county Regional Transportation District—the great sensible middle—weren't afforded the opportunity to perceive light rail in a clear-sighted way—in a way that simultaneously 1) championed rail and 2) respected taxpayer pocketbooks. To iterate, voters had been denied acquaintance with a couple of fundamental truths. RTD can fund a comprehensive light-rail system without an increase in its current 0.6 percent sales tax—and complete the job within a tolerable time span.

There was never anything in the hater/lover relationship to suggest a conscious conspiracy. Remaining resolutely itself, each group interacted with the other just fine without resorting to clandestine meetings and secret handshakes. The haters were merely doing what came naturally and winning. The lovers were overreacting and losing, as those with unruly zeal often do, falling prey to the law of unintended consequences.

Three Strikes You're Out

Tax elections have come and gone in the district—three of them—without laying any rapid transit. The first in 1973 passed rather handily, but as discussed in Chapter 5 officials violated their political vow, failing to devote any part of the proceeds to rail. What's almost as bad, no official ever bothered to deal publicly with the failure—with the issue of why the tax wasn't rescinded (as had been repeatedly promised) when RTD didn't do what it said it would.[1]

The second tax-increase election came in 1980, the same year voters decided to oust the appointed board and replace it with an elected board. This proposal went down to defeat by a vote of 54 to 46 percent, with opinion polls suggesting two reasons. For one thing, the request for a 0.75 percentage-point jump struck voters as too big a bite from the apple. For another, there were more than a few citizens who at the time harbored intensely bitter feelings against RTD. Disgruntled voters sorely resented both the third-rate service they encountered on the streets and the recurrent episodes of financial high-handedness they read about in the papers and heard about on their radios.

Before commenting on how the third tax election degenerated into the biggest bust of all, it's necessary to fast-forward some eight years. By this time, 1997, RTD found itself in a bubbling kettle of good feelings, bad feelings and fractious disagreement. Its inaugural 5.3-mile MAC was up and running to widespread hurrahs, and construction had begun on the 9.8-mile Southwest Corridor extension. Numerous citizens nonetheless worried that traffic congestion was rapidly approaching the tripping point, especially along the Southeast Corridor from I-25 and Broadway to the Technological Center. Further, the board had fractured itself into unabashed covens of light-rail haters and lovers.[2]

Goaded and Egged

Goaded by the Denver Metro Chamber of Commerce and egged on by GM Cal Marsella, who hid a limited imagination and mediocre skills under a bushel of political spin and personal hype, the board decided to bring the expansion question to a public vote on 7 November 1997. An awkward and derivative patchwork of transport projects financed by a 0.4 percentage-point sales-tax hike, the proposition was something voters found easy to reject. This they proceeded to do by a landslide 58 to 42 percent.

Frenziedly supporting the measure, as is its posture with regard to virtually every consumer tax hike, The Denver Post lambasted all those rash enough to venture disagreement, casting aspersions on their character and family life as well as their intelligence. Its editors propounded the blinkered doctrine "everything-at-once" as the one and only way to go.

The Rocky Mountain News on the other hand opposed the tax issue, thanks almost entirely to its then-publisher Larry D. Strutton. No lover or hater he but a person of moderate outlook, Strutton supported light rail, especially along the Southeast Corridor to the Technological Center. An old-school gentlemen and quick study, Strutton wanted light rail put in play as soon and as effectively as possible. While his paper had editorially opposed building the first line, the 5.3-mile MAC, it had undergone a change of opinion after evaluating the project in action. The News now favored an incremental buildout without tax boosts.

Hunt for Scapegoats

To lovers and their wide circle of allied enthusiasts, the public defeat delivered a head-snapping shock. And they began casting about for an easy-to-target scapegoat even before all the votes were counted.

They blamed in particular Director John Caldera (O) who led the vocal opposition, plus a generally divided board of directors. Their cause would have been better served had they let up just a little on their designated scapegoats and looked inside the impoverished proposition they had set before the voting public, a proposition chock-a-block with its own seeds of defeat. The negative vote wasn't against rail, but against greed. The proposal sank primarily because voters viewed it as misconceived, lacking in focus and shamefully grabby. History had repeated itself. The smother-lovers had just revalidated Walt Kelly's famous maxim to the effect: "We have met the enemy and he is us."

Did the lessons take hold? Hardly. After taking the same tack several times over and enduring the same rejection again and again, the Chamber crowd and its RTD confederates readied themselves to adopt the same threadbare approach: They remained stubbornly intent on trying to build in all directions at once. This was a humongous mistake.

The truth: There were no fundamental reasons for the all-or-nothing way of looking at things. Voters didn't want it; there were no redeeming economics of scale; the necessary money wasn't at hand. The question needing exploration was "Does the community want a little something or a whole lot of nothing?" The common-sense response and, for most residents, the preferable answer by far was a little "something," especially when the "something" carried the potential for considerably more later on.

It was getting quite old, as country singer Patty Loveless says, "forever replacing hope with regret." The next time around light-rail extension should be promoted in a way that's doable and responsive to voter desires. Light rail should be built incrementally—one step at a time.

Public Funding Limited

True, not every governmental undertaking readily lends itself to segmentation, but rapid transit virtually demands a step-by-step strategy. Not only should light rail be implemented one section at a time, but taxpayers should retain the right to pull the plug whenever they want, for whatever reasons they might choose.

As distasteful as the foregoing doubtlessly seems to more than a few palpitating light-rail fans, it warranted appreciative acceptance by most metro-area residents. What's more, scarce public monies propelled discussion in the same direction. Thus did limited public funding demonstrate an upside. It added middle-of-the-road horse-sense to endless and often pointless palaver.

Here's a brief rundown on where public financing stood after the 1997 defeat: The 0.4 percentage-point sales-tax hike that RTD called "Guide the Ride" lay stone-cold dead in the minds of the electorate. It was unlikely to be resurrected any time soon. That meant:

- Metro-area voters had decided they would not construct a comprehensive light-rail system in the foreseeable future.

- But they left RTD free to build a system one route at a time.

The two points joined together yield a valuable insight: Although voters had firmly rejected all tax-hike requests, they never, ever rejected light rail itself. Consequently RTD felt in no way deterred from forging ahead with incremental extensions—just so long as these extensions imposed no new taxes.

To elaborate just a bit, voters wanted light rail—clamored for it even—but didn't want it badly enough to pay higher sales taxes in order to get it. Looking at first blush like an untenable demand for a free lunch, the position is in truth entirely reasonable. For one thing, there's nothing inherently illogical or immoral about wanting improved products for the same or even less money. For another, the provision of new and better goods and services without higher real prices is the recorded history of developed economies during the past millennium. Especially during the 1990s, well within the personal experience of most readers, better products of sundry size, shape and usefulness arrived at market almost everywhere at stable or declining prices.

Middle-Class Comfort

The question of whether rail can be introduced and expanded without higher taxes (prices) constitutes a matter of fact, not theory. And what do the facts have to say? They answer the query affirmatively. Thanks to the dynamic growth in its revenues over the past decade or so (see Illustration III on page 92), RTD has climbed from the straightened circumstances in which it dwelled through the early and middle 1980s to solid middle-class comfort. Though not luxuriating in champagne and sable—as would have been its sumptuous fortune had the 1997 tax referendum succeeded—RTD achieved a level of prosperity high enough to allow it to set aside something for investment at the same time it continued to provide reasonably good bus service.

Progressive companies and prudent families have worked the economic system in precisely this way since the days of yore—to the benefit of both themselves and their communities. Vladimir Ilyick Lenin didn't particularly admire those who participated in the process, calling them "blood-sucking capitalists" and "petty bourgeoisie." But then Lenin, although still entombed in lonely splendor in Moscow's Red Square, is no longer viewed even in Russia as a fount of economic wisdom.

By using these financial set asides—5 to 10 percent of current revenues—to borrow in national capital markets, taking full advantage of differentially low local-government interest rates, RTD could commence building a full-fledged light-rail system immediately. There was no compelling reason why not. Sadly, however, there was a convenient excuse not to do so—the partly mindless and partly gluttonous and wholly crippling political fixation on building everything at once.

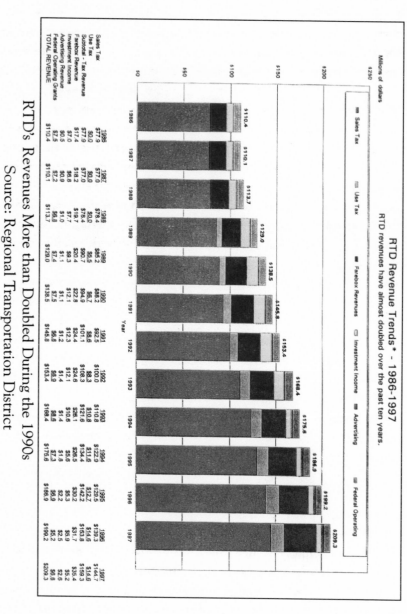

RTD's Revenues More than Doubled During the 1990s

Source: Regional Transportation District

Illustration III

Success Brings New Problems

When RTD began thinking seriously about breaking ground for its 5.3-mile MAC, it smacked into what appeared to be an impregnable barrier. Although light rail lit fires of enthusiasm under many citizens, scarcely anybody was willing to put up with light rail tracking through his or her own neighborhood. A curious discrepancy this—one that led those of us then working the project to this conclusion: If the day ever comes, we agreed, when residents start jockeying with one another over whose backyard gets the next line, RTD will know for sure that it has sired a winner. Well, the day arrived almost immediately. Soon after the MAC's maiden run, RTD had a real contender on its hands.

But success brought new problems. RTD came under heavy pressure from various groups to take the next line in six directions—Northwest, North, East, Southeast, West and into Platte Valley. The problem? RTD lacked the money and capacity and know-how to box the compass. As to the dream of building every-which-way-at-once, it was a snare and delusion, and simply not in the tarot pack. Much of what RTD needed to do at the time was pick the corridor it considered the most promising.

Seemingly crystal clear, the principles undergirding the selection process: one, go where the needs are the greatest; two, where the chances for success seem best; and three, where the outlook for financing is most favorable. These indicators then need double-checking against reality, using both on-site observation and econometric modeling.

Southeast Front-Runner

Neither test left any doubt about the direction RTD ought to head out. Everyday experience revealed the Southeast Corridor to the Technological Center suffered the worst congestion and also provided the best opportunity for success. RTD's numerous econometric and statistical studies added corroborative evidence.[3]

While the 19.6-mile Southeast Corridor led the pack by several furlongs in the race for initial construction, RTD directors regularly reminded themselves about traffic congestion in other areas. Indeed, some board members recognized early on that the shortest route to overall funding lay in first building an undeniable success—a blockbuster if possible. And if a genuine smash hit wasn't possible, then they should build something that could at least lead citizens to reflect on light rail benignly.

Another reason some board members accepted the Southeast Corridor as the front-runner: It could be put into place for about half the per-passenger outlays required by the alternatives. The advantage stemmed from exceptionally vigorous demand along the route and from the fact that 20 percent of the line was already up-and-running.[4]

How much would it cost to complete the Southeast line? In round numbers $850 million. Could RTD generate the money without a tax increase? Relatively easily and in ways that would foster a fast start. By devoting $20 million of its annual revenues—about 5 percent of current income—to bond repayments, RTD could raise more than $400 million in immediately spendable monies—enough to cover all local requirements.

The remainder could come from the federal government—about $400 million. RTD would find this sum sufficient. Washington would almost certainly find it agreeable.

More Than One Way

Are there other paths that could have been followed? Of course. "Two roads diverged in a wood and I—I followed the less traveled by. And that has made all the difference." Thus go Robert Frost's best-known lines, his most famous because they resonate so broadly.[5] There's always more than one way to tell a story or swing a cat, and pretty obviously there's more than one way to pay for light rail.

But at the time this was the quickest and most practical way to move ahead. Quite possibly it was the only way in the short run. Legions of elected officials, however, including some board members, sternly rejected the approach. They proposed waiting the recalcitrants out. "Hold on," they urged, and state officials together with federal officials will serve up everything RTD wants on a silver-plated platter—not just for the Southeast Corridor but for an entire 100-mile system as well.[6]

Such assumptions really do lead nowhere—they suggest that great good fortune awaits in the ambient air; that next week our ship will come in, or that manna from heaven will drop into our indolent laps. RTD had tried waiting on total federal funding before and had found that real-life doesn't work like that. (This was in fact RTD's first really big mistake. See Chapter 7 for a detailed explanation.)

No Loitering Allowed

Playing the lottery is permissible and hope is essential to life. But these truisms provide no reason to turn blue-sky foolhardy.

Should such will-o'-the-wisp funds actually flow RTD's way then all the better. Such funding could be put to good use in putting together a comprehensive mix of trains, buses and auto-mobile lanes—a unified system that should be assembled over the long run. And let it ring abundantly clear that the "long run" in this context doesn't mean the "long run in which we are all dead" as British economist John Maynard Keynes remarked decades ago. It meant, at the most, 15 to 25 years.[7]

Loitering around putting off work that needs to be done today is terribly defeatist and altogether bad strategic policy. How hard should it be, really, for public officials to appreciate the need to move forward with the people's business as promptly and as cost-effectively as possible?

Notes

1. RTD officials apparently went into the 1973 election hoping Washington would kick in the major portion of the needed funding. Washington not only did not but presumably never intended to. Metro Denver citizens were the only ones fooled into thinking it might.
2. John Caldera (O) led the haters; Karen Benker (M) led the lovers. Only Gloria Holliday (B) and Jack McCroskey (A) avoided identification with either group. On leaving RTD, Caldera became president of the Golden-based Independence Institute, a free-market and implacably anti-light-rail think tank. Benker retained her position as a mid-level state civil servant.
3. Over the past several decades RTD had commissioned more than $20 million in mainly useless studies. If there was ever an instance of the map being mistaken for the territory this was it. Studies as often as not were viewed as an end in themselves.
4. The 20 percent was thanks to the Central Corridor which was originally located so it could serve as the first leg of built out lines in all directions: southwest, southeast, east, north and so on. See Illustration I and pages 84-86.
5. Robert Frost, "The Road Not Taken," *Early Poems*, NY; Penguin Books, 1998.
6. Leading advocates for this point of view in intra-board debates were: Mary Blue (I) and Dick McLean (O). Both Blue and McLean vigorously supported light rail but neither supported the idea of building a system incrementally.
7. John Maynard Keynes, *General Theory of Employment, Interest and Money*, NY; Harcourt Brace, 1936.

10
LEGISLATIVE AMBUSH
The Board Pulls Out a Cliffhanger

State Senator Sandy Hume of Boulder (R) and State Representative Kathy Williams of Westminster (R) were bound, determined and blithely confident. The MAC would never see sunshine.

How could they be so sure?

Rather routine members of the legislature themselves, Hume and Williams had an ace in the hole: The ambitious and determinedly effective State Senator Bill Owens—a Republican whose vocation and destiny it was to assume in year 1999 the governorship from Democrat Roy Romer. With Owens solidly behind them Hume and Williams seemed assured of getting something anti-MAC past the legislature. Their only real apprehension: Governor Romer might decide to invoke his veto.

But shouldn't a Romer veto fall into the "certain" category rather than hover above the fray as a mere possibility? Unlike Owens, who candidly admitted disliking light rail as much as his Fort Worth homefolks disdain the folks in Dallas, Romer professed abiding devotion. And a veto of the Hume/Williams bill would lift light rail into near-term certainty.

The answer in brief: No, Romer wasn't about to take up his veto pen, partly because like other rail extremists he considered the MAC too paltry to bother with. Thus an anti-MAC bill could slide across his desk in perfect safety. Again, and with no need for prior powwows (although the author cannot swear there weren't any), hate and love pooled their powers to harass and possibly upend light rail.

And no mistake about it the purpose here was to thwart the MAC. So despite the RTD board's strenuous efforts and with the three essential legs firmly in place, it began to look as if rail might be heading straight for the junkyard. Powerful politicians had taken the issue to an entirely different level.

Senate Bill 208

To begin the new game, Hume and Williams identified a legislative bill they could readily use—a bill already percolating through the current session (1991) and one with a commodious title.[1] This turned out to be Senate Bill 208.

They then bided their time until three days before the General Assembly adjourned—the wait here being crucial. During the last three days of Colorado legislative sessions, rules requiring opportunities for public input into pending laws are suspended. Thus do bills sneak through loopholes and into state statute books without critical analysis and public viewing.

Finally Hume and Williams amended Senate Bill 208 in ways that suited their purposes and persuaded the General Assembly to pass it—the Senate by 22 to 12; the House by 34 to 30. All this took place under the cover of statehouse darkness. Neither RTD officials nor citizens nor voters received a heads up as to what was actually happening. Owens, as he later told his legislative colleagues, believed the bill would bury light rail once and for all.

Owens had plenty of reason to think interment would occur posthaste. Senate Bill 208 had shoved the MAC into the muck, and there were plenty of heavy lifters around to handle the digging. Among the muscular gentry were Governor Roy Romer, the General Assembly, Denver Mayor Federico Peña, Aurora Mayor Paul Tauer, the Metro Denver Chamber, the Denver Partnership, the *Rocky Mountain News*, plus sundry others, including a bunch of talk-show hosts and newspaper columnists.

New Restraints

Like a lightning zap from Zeus, passage of Senate Bill 208 caught RTD by surprise, leaving the board perched on the edge of a steep precipice with tough options to consider. The easiest would have been to tip light rail over the side and let it splatter on the rocks below. Who would have experienced shock? Who would have suffered depression? Very few ordinary citizens and virtually no political operatives. Ho-hum. Yawn. Just more RTD folderol.

The gutsy option—the one chosen with scarcely a pause and with few illusions about the difficulties ahead—was for the board to try its very best to overcome the restraints state government had just imposed. These new obstacles were:

• The number of board votes required to begin building rail lines jumped from eight out of 15 (a simple majority) to ten of 15 (a two-thirds majority).

• The Denver Regional Council of Governments (DRCOG)[2] received authority to kill RTD rail starts by majority vote. Authority here did not extend to allowing DRCOG to begin rail lines or even offer suggestions about where new lines might be located. DRCOG's new powers allowed it to do just one thing, exact the death penalty.

State government for various reasons had put a stopper in the light-rail bottle and fully intended that it not come out.[3] The RTD board on the other hand, firmly believed this was the time and place to begin.

The board saw only one way to prevail. It must convince DRCOG to say yes. And the best way to do this, the board believed, was to talk things over with DRCOG members.

Lakewood (Pop. 144,126). The first DRCOG member we spoke to—Mayor Linda Morton and City Council members—greeted the proposal with indulgence. A rail start, they agreed, even a diminutive one of 1.7 miles, would represent a giant step forward. Their response breathed new spirit into the proceedings but also left a profoundly false notion about what lay ahead.

For a moment the board imagined itself indulging in a euphoric stroll through fields of columbines. Wrong flowers, wrong type of outing. The board soon found itself trapped in another marathon—one pocked with political and racist hazards.

Englewood (Pop. 31,727). The most unpleasant and unnerving group on the itinerary, Englewood City Council members disliked everything about the proposal. The line was too short; it cost way too much; it touched down in Five Points; nobody would ever use it. Some council members cranked up their opposition into overkill, phoning the author at home (I was RTD chairman at the time) threatening personal and professional damage as vengeance for promoting something they saw as so Rube Goldberg.

Much later, with nary a reference to these early encounters, Englewood Mayor Tom Burns would seek public congratulations for his town's enlightened encouragement of light rail and for its magnanimous help in fathering same. He's at it still.

Denver (Pop. 554,636). One of the biggest problems with Denver Mayor Federico Peña: During the half-dozen or so meetings with him and his staff, he could never bring himself to utter either the word "yes" or the word "no." Equally galling was his habit of suggesting—in a pinched-nose sort of way—that RTD leadership wasn't quite up to snuff. The project itself might—just might—turn out to be marginally beneficial some day, but he really couldn't commit himself, partly because the sad sacks from RTD couldn't hold their own in discussions with either himself or his dynamite staff.[4]

Several years later, after Peña had become President Bill Clinton's Secretary of Transportation, he came home again bearing a "full funding agreement" designed to provide federal money for the MAC's Littleton extension.[5] During the presentation ceremony (de rigueur for such occasions) he pointedly cold-shouldered everybody who had anything constructive to do with welding together the MAC.

Aurora (Pop. 276,393). It wasn't that Aurora Mayor Paul Tauer disliked light rail as a far-off dream, he just couldn't brook the notion of starting with a demonstration line in the middle of downtown Denver. (And especially he couldn't bear the thought of a line running anywhere near the African-American neighborhood of Five Points.) Somewhat myopically and despite the issue having been argued many times, he simply could not foresee MAC extensions ever reaching his own community, located some ten miles east of central Denver.

Although exceptionally popular Tauer didn't prevail on this one. A City Council majority disagreed and Aurora voted "aye" when the issue came before DRCOG. A light-rail line is currently making its way to Aurora as part of the Southeast-Corridor expansion, and Paul Tauer is actively campaigning for big hikes in light-rail taxes.

Sales Presentation

So it went for many moons and upwards of 300 presentations to mayors, city councils, county commissioners, political parties, taxpayer associations, neighborhood groups, college classes, business organizations, newspapers, service clubs. A grueling and picaresque journey through Colorado's urban heart. Some of the trip proved painful and some seemed pleasant, but before long the effort grew a little tedious since the sales pitch amounted to recycling basically the same thoughts at each and every gathering. To wit:

• We have the opportunity today to build a light-rail demonstration line. After 25 years of black-and-blue head-butting, let's give light rail a chance.

• We will hereby redeem in a small way the promise made so many years ago when RTD was just getting under way. Remember that promise? It was to build a rapid-transit system within the revenues generated by RTD's 0.6 percent sales tax.

• If citizens don't like the results, then the dispute will grind to a halt and the community can direct its attention to more urgent topics. If citizens are pleased, then this demonstration line built as the spine of a prospective system will serve as the first leg for extensions in every direction.

Some groups seemed immediately amenable; others came across as harshly dismissive. Leaving aside these extremes, most middle-roaders seemed desirous but dubious. They wanted to forge ahead but were held back by two misgivings. One concerned the provincial question of if and when a line would ever reach their own neighborhoods. The other involved Five Points. Many couldn't comprehend why this neighborhood was included in a demonstration project.

No Guarantees

The board would have promised to spread out lines in all directions if it could have. But this the board could not do in good faith. So to the question "What comes after the MAC?" the answer had to be: "No one can say for sure, but here are three possibilities":

• Citizens find they don't particularly like light rail. The MAC stays on as a stand-alone line. Probability? Low.

• Citizens welcome light rail with sheer delight, finding it an attractive congestion-busting, cost-effective way to promote mobility. They celebrate by raising sales taxes to build an entire system as quickly as possible. Probability? Middling.

• Citizens like light rail very much but reject the burden of higher taxes. RTD moves to expand the system in measured ways, using federal funds, bus savings and the natural revenue gains that flow from price increases and economic growth—that is, increases in population and productivity. Probability? High.

The board wasn't able to underwrite the future (only a charlatan would so claim) but no one should have doubted that rail systems can start small and expand prudently. Note the one-mile cable-car beginning in San Francisco (see Chapter 1) and the Boston subway system which emerged before the turn of the 20th century with a one-mile trolley under its Commons. Where there's a will in matters of public transport, there is also a way.

Bigotry Covert and Overt

"Why are you going to Five Points?" It wasn't a question, not really. Some of the literally thousands who posed it may have actually wanted specific information but the vast majority did not. For most questioners, the query represented euphemistically phrased resentment against taking light rail into a relatively low-income African-American neighborhood.

To put the matter bluntly, it was bigotry masquerading as curiosity. The author has heard and seen enough and been around enough during his almost 80 years to recognize bigotry when he encounters it. This was bigotry. The tone and inflection with which the questions were usually asked underscored that fact. So did the more than occasional ruffles in the majority community's politically placid surface. The DRCOG delegate from the upscale southeastern suburb of Greenwood Village, for instance, voiced unabashed complaints to the effect that light rail going into Five Points would be used primarily for illegal drug trafficking. Others moaned that bringing "them" down in carload lots would push up crime rates in largely white southeast Denver. Let the author hasten to announce that these ugly forecasts proved worse than merely wrong. They proved surpassingly ignorant.

What such covert and overt bigotry could have done—and in fact came within a hair's breath of actually doing—was choke off Denver's first light-rail line. Had bigotry succeeded with its usual mischief, America would have suffered one more loss to segregation and discrimination.

Swedish sociologist Gunner Myrdal long ago laid out with great clarity in his groundbreaking two-volume *An American Dilemma: The Negro Problem and Modern Democracy* (1942) the enormous costs the sins of discrimination impose on society as a whole.[6] Economics Nobel Laureate Gary Becker detailed these losses more precisely during the 1960s by likening them to external tariffs.[7] Sadly many Denverites remained serenely oblivious to these well-documented conclusions. Some poor souls simply could not visualize humanity across the racial divide—a common type of social blindness that Ralph Ellison dissected in his masterfully written and broadly influential novel of 1952, *The Invisible Man*.[8]

Foothold

In the meantime, state legislators continued their sniping. Among the most memorable potshots: State Senator Al Meiklejohn (R), a tall and cadaverous-looking attorney, almost broke up a joint legislative committee by calling yours truly "totally insane" for even entertaining such an idiotic proposal.[9] (He clearly intended his remarks as a clinical diagnosis rather than an insult.) But even Meiklejohn, as he reached the agitated peak of his outrage, managed to sound an undeniable truth: "The

RTD staff had absolutely nothing to do with any of this," he exploded. "The board of directors is responsible. The board is the culprit."

The conflicting currents and broken promises, shifting positions and mixed motives—added together these made it altogether impossible to predict with any confidence how the final vote would play out on the evening of 17 July 1991 when DRCOG rendered its final decision.

The sighs of relief and whoops of jubilation heard throughout DRCOG's capacious offices tolled the victory. The MAC had won the battle by 20 to 15 roll-call votes. Light rail had secured a firm foothold. Underdogs had beaten the long odds against them and pulled out a cliffhanger. Building light rail could at long last get started. After so many years of frustration, the breakthrough was exhilarating for light-rail fans across the district.

CAUTIONARY NOTE

The word "build" can be more than a little misleading when associated with RTD. Do not imagine that RTD's senior staff personally engineers or constructs the agency's light-rail plant and equipment. What it does in fact with board approval is hire competent private contractors who in turn employ and supervise the skilled technicians and craftspeople who engage in the actual engineering and construction.

Notes

1. Titles for bills in the Colorado General Assembly cannot be expanded to cover additional items after introduction. Thus a bill titled "RTD Sales Tax" cannot go beyond these taxes, while a bill titled "Concerning RTD" can be amended to deal with anything relating to RTD.

2. DRCOG is a voluntary planning association made up of local governments from within the Denver Metropolitan District. A public but non-governmental agency, it serves as a vehicle for intergovernmental cooperation.

3. The General Assembly could hamstring RTD's efforts to build the MAC but it didn't dare forbid building outright. RTD's legal right to construct rail using existing tax revenues had been granted in a popular plebiscite. The legislature has always been loath to overturn a public vote.

4. Mayor Peña's Director of Community Planning, Frank Gray, scoffed at the usefulness of a downtown starter line. He urged instead: Build the 15 miles or so from Stapleton Airport on the city's eastern edge to soon-to-open DIA. Gray simply would not allow himself to believe that RTD hadn't the funds to go 15 miles. Nor could he accept RTD's stated objective to begin with a multi-purpose line—a line that could serve as both demonstration and full-system centerpiece. At this point in time, Mayor Peña's administration appeared gung-ho for anything considered helpful to DIA and lethargically blasé about everything else.

5. A written agreement between the federal executive branch and a local government wherein the federal agency guarantees the local government a specified amount toward the completion of a specific project. Congress must still appropriate the funds and may change the timing of payments, but it is generally assumed that the total amount promised will be forthcoming.

6. Gunner Myrdal, *American Dilemma*, NY; Harper Collins Publishing, 1944.

7. Gary Spence Becker, *The Economics of Discrimination*, Chicago; University of Chicago Press, 1957.

8. Ralph Ellison, *The Invisible Man*, NY; Random House Publishing, 1952.
9. This is just a wee bit ironic—a senatorial grandee labeling the author "insane" for undertaking Denver's first light-rail line. Assistant GM John Caflin, with GM Marsella's full approval, calls the author "crazy" for just the opposite reason—for thinking he had anything to do with building the first line. Go figure.

11

BUILDING A SYSTEM
The Little Train That Could

Rail Line	Opening Date
5.3-mile MAC Corridor	*Oct. 7, 1994*
8.7-mile Southwest Corridor	*July 14, 2000*
1.8-mile Platte Valley Corridor	*April 5, 2002*
19.6-mile Southeast Corridor	*Planned 2006*

A total of 35.4 miles either in operation or ready to go politically and financially. The 20-mile East Corridor to Denver International Airport (DIA) can be built without tax increases.

The MAC opening, 7 October 1994, came on big and happy—as big almost as a Super Bowl win by the Denver Broncos and as rollicking as a Judy Garland chorus of "Clang, Clang, Clang Goes the Trolley."[1]

Good-natured crowds of a thousand and more thronged the stations and later packed the cars as tightly as New York City's subways during rush hours. Some passengers expressed their satisfaction with smiles and congratulations. Others simply enjoyed the whisper-smooth rides, punctuating their pleasure with audible "oohs" and "aahs." Although in truth, owing to unseasoned drivers overusing their emergency brakes, these early riders felt more leaping and lurching than would be experienced later on.

But the system as a whole performed as promised, with on-board air-conditioning deserving special notice. The cool—almost cold—air proved a godsend during the warm October afternoons of opening weeks when virtually every train ran full to the gunnels.

From 5.0 to 1.7 to 5.3

At this high-point in the tale of "How Light Rail Came to Denver" the author feels reluctantly compelled to interrupt his-torical continuity with a brief flashback explaining how a 5.0 mile proposal shrank to 1.7 miles during middle passage and then jumped back to 5.3 miles at opening.

Up, down, up—the abrupt changes left observers bewildered. "Why can't you make up your minds?" they asked—which was not only a fair question, but one the board tried to answer at the time. That it failed to do so convincingly stemmed more from dirt-devils kicked up by the media than from a lack of good intentions. Either way, confusion continues to reign. So the author here ventilates what wasn't fully explained early on: exactly how the seesaw confusion arose and how the matter finally played out.

Starting with earnest preparations for building 5.0 miles, RTD ran almost immediately into a destructive headwind, with the original plan dropping to 1.7 miles when hit by Hurricane NIMBY (see Chapter 7). More than an inconvenience, the gusts here howled strongly enough to scupper the entire project. A 5.0-mile line would allow rail vehicles to sail along at 50 miles per hour on grade-separated guideways; a 1.7-mile line could not. The shrunken line would demonstrate light-rail cars navigating their way through crowded city streets without disrupting traffic or upsetting normal life, but it couldn't show them at their workaday job of ferrying lots of people freely and easily through-out the metropolitan area.

Building a 1.7-mile line would get light rail started to be sure. But would a bare start be enough to capture public attention and imagination? Would it foster additional building? There was as much to be said against the possibility as in favor.[2] At best begin-ning with a line so severely shortened would be to flirt with the danger of a public-relations trouncing.

Decision Time Again

So how should the board react? Throw in the towel? Such could have happened. Refined intelligence as well as common sense—a smattering of each—counseled the board to abandon the entire project.

Roll with the punches? Sensible or not, something deep and prodding (probably pride and defiance) told the board it had come too far to back out now. So what was finally decided was to take the plunge and go after DRCOG's approval of the 1.7-mile segment (see Chapter 8). With this OK firmly in hand, we could then circle back and figure out how to assemble a revamped project—something both taxpayers and users would find more palatable.

In seeking a second approval so soon after the first, the board was keenly aware that it needed to offer DRCOG members an exceptionally succulent plum, an opportunity so attractive it couldn't be refused. As it happened an irresistible deal stood readily at hand. We could proffer a 3.6-mile extension that over the long haul would not cost anything at all. To some suspicious citizens the idea of light-rail freebies appeared farcical but the figures were nonetheless sound and true. The additional 3.6 miles could be had entirely gratis.

Marginal Cost and Present Value

The new presentation called for the adroit employment of two widely used concepts, both economic in nature: marginal costs and present value.[3] Although slandered by a few critics as a sleight-of-hand exercise in financial hugger-mugger, the presentation aimed in fact at straightforward demonstration. It went like this:

• RTD's first light-rail line, the Metro Area Connection (MAC), will run from 30th Avenue and Downing through the Five Points business area and downtown Denver, by the Auraria campus and then along railroad right-of-way to I-25 and Broadway (see Illustration II, page 79).

• Funded entirely by RTD, no tax increase and no federal dollars are needed. The northern segment between Downing and Auraria campus will be paid for with RTD's existing sales-and-use tax ($70 million) and has already received DRCOG approval.

• The marginal or additional cost of the 3.6-mile southern segment between Auraria campus and I-25/Broadway will be financed wholly by the present (capitalized) value of taking approximately 500 bus trips per day off city streets. (Bus service replaced by rail service.)

• Because the rail-repair facility and most of the cars were counted in the costs of the original project, the 3.6-mile southern segment between Auraria campus and I-25 /Broadway amounts to just $30 million, less than one-fourth the per-mile cost assigned to the first 1.7 miles.

• Present value of the saving in deleted bus trips also amounts to $30 million. Thus, the 3.6 mile extension costs nothing over the long run. (See Appendix E for the original presentation.)

Less Skittish the Second Time Around

If you liked the original line, the board told DRCOG, you'll adore the new one. And it was in fact much easier to drum up support the second time around, reflecting in part the universal appeal of something for nothing.

Another reason for the less skittish response lay in the gathering belief that light rail could start small and grow vastly larger, extending ultimately from its centerpiece across the entire district. Adding a little color to the conviction, board members repeatedly related the remarkably prescient comment Benjamin Franklin made long ago about the chair George Washington sat on during the 1787 Constitutional Convention in Philadelphia.

Franklin studied that chair, with an ambiguous sun carved into its back, throughout the proceedings. Then as the meeting wound down, Franklin sagely observed, "Now I'm convinced. The sun on the General's chair is rising, not setting."

The MAC, too, seemed ascendant. DRCOG voted in favor of the extension by 30 to 15, with the winning margin here running considerably larger than that scored in the first tally. RTD celebrated forthwith by incorporating a fierce morning sun into its first light-rail logo,[4] as shown in Illustration IV below.

Myth Versus Real Thing

Finally and thoroughly ready to go, Denver light rail now faced the greatest challenge of all. How many people would continue to ride after the opening hoopla died down? Hopes ran high—although no one had any assurances of what lay ahead and despite the fact that ridership forecasts for new light-rail lines across the country had proved notoriously inflated, with predictions often exceeding actual counts by huge percentages. Further the US Department of Transportation had only recently released a glibly damning report purporting to reveal a nationwide pattern of light-rail failure.[5]

But Denver turned out differently. Rail supporters weren't disappointed, they were overjoyed. Passenger boardings outpaced expectations on day one and then galloped ahead through succeeding years by whopping 30 to 50-percent margins.

The pessimism bedeviling Colorado light rail for so long could be blamed partly on cowboy mythology—the sort of western chimera that best-selling novelist Larry McMurtry said he had tried but failed to debunk in his Pulitzer Prize winning *Lonesome Dove* (1958).[6] "The romance of the West is so powerful that you really can't swim against the current," McMurtry commented "Whatever truth about the West is printed, the legend is always more powerful."

The University of Colorado's Patricia Nelson Limerick, both the deepest thinker and sharpest writer in New Western History, laments that mythologizing has made it all but impossible for Westerners to achieve self-knowledge. "Try to write realistically about the Old West and what you write will be condemned as gloomy or disillusioning."[7] The latter-day cowboy mania (Roy Rogers, Hopalong Cassidy, Marshal Dillon and their buffoonish sidekicks) had passed its high-watermark by the early 1970s but many Colorado Front Range voters appeared nonetheless bound by visions of a lone rider, tall in the saddle with six-guns in his holster and a 20-gauge shotgun over his shoulder, roaming open range through Marlboro Country.

What McMurtry and Limerick argue is that Marlboro Country doesn't exist and never did.[8] Sadly, their writings have done little to alter the mind-set of those gripped by the fantasy and less still to shake up stagnant public policy—all of which is unfortunate but scarcely surprising since not too many people experience an epiphany upon ingesting a book or so. All too many observers, both ordinary citizens and policymakers, continued to view Westerners through a Ponderosa prism, seeing them as too independent and too self-reliant to patronize light rail. It took the MAC demonstration line to begin turning public perception around. Helped by extensive word-of-mouth advertising, crowded park-and-ride lots plus eye-popping ridership statistics turned the trick.

Varieties of Desire

Another factor aggravating delays in light-rail development: The deep-seated belief that automobile addiction cannot be mitigated. Maybe an analogy with the cigarette habit can help sort out the issue.

Cigarettes are terribly hard to vanquish—as hard perhaps as heroin or crack cocaine. One reason is that cigarettes cater to so many varieties of desire. Aside from delivering nicotine, they serve as companions and appetite suppressors. They steady the nerves and promise physical and emotional lifts. They appeal to many senses: touch, taste, sight, smell—and to some men and women and children, they add a frisson of glamour. You don't see it too much anymore but not too long ago movie stars with all their extraordinary authority and influence couldn't cut a scene without lighting, inhaling, extinguishing or just fondling pseudosophisticated smokes.

But despite its hard-core allure, the cigarette habit has fallen in consumer favor, with smokers dropping from 50 to 25 percent of the US population between 1965 and 2000.[9] Cynics didn't believe a reversal like this could occur. Neither did most romantics. But astonishingly, not to say miraculously, the scarcely believable has come to pass.

Changing Fashions

Automobiles possess lures and hooks of their own. Convenience and the ability to accommodate highly individualistic travel agendas head the list. But automobiles also represent a style, a look, an attitude, a ubiquitous way of showing off—none of which the author considers in any way wrong or deserving censure.[10]

The significant point: Both convenience and style are relative affairs. As public transport extends service and as city streets grow increasingly confining, relative convenience narrows between public transport and private automobiles. Moreover, as fashions change-and fashion walks hand-in-hand with trendiness—

attitudes toward the style of the moment also change. Just as appetites for cigarettes can ricochet, so can tastes for automobiles. Who knows, before long public transport may become socially prestigious—maybe even cool.[11]

One thing most certainly: Individuals can derive psychological benefits from both *not* smoking and *not* driving. Add the positives of not driving to the positives of taking transit and the stage seems set for gains in public transport's market share. And the gains will almost certainly prove substantial as light rail becomes increasingly accessible. No doubt about it, new tastes need not await cataclysmic developments—the emergence of a Soviet-type "New Man" or a generation screened by galatonian eugenics. Nor is there any reason to hold off until the biotechnical revolution takes off. Shifts in urban travel preferences are even now picking up considerable speed.

As regards overall population, the fight against smoking faces a much tougher war than does the fight against traffic congestion. While anti-tobacco crusaders won't celebrate until the last evil leaf has been consigned to perdition, anti-congestion fighters seek only a reduction in automobile usage. No sensible person wants automobiles purged from urban life. Regular folks don't hate automobiles, not literally. Realists don't expect Americans will voluntarily give up automobile ownership.

What a large portion of Americans can do is conserve just a little on urban driving. Some may conserve a lot. These changes can go a long way toward easing chronic congestion. A 25 percentage-point drop in urban-miles-driven—the same drop as with cigarette smokers—would be embraced as a monumental victory in the battle against traffic congestion. Even much smaller declines will be heartily welcomed.[9]

From 1.7 to 35.4 Miles

The MAC was built to be used, and it has been used very well—first, as a demonstration line for citizens who weren't acquainted with light rail; second, as a heavily patronized central-city connector; and, third, as the centerpiece from which rail lines can be built linking the entire six-county transportation district. The MAC has served quite effectively in these respects, as a sample and as a productive stepping stone. No one on the RTD board at the time expected things to work out otherwise. No one—least of all the author—ever imagined the MAC as light rail's *Alpha* and *Omega*.

As successful as its most ambitious advocates could have wished, the MAC has yielded an abundantly healthy harvest, up from 1.7 track miles under way in 1992 to 35.4 miles in 2003, either in operation or under construction. Compare this outcome with the results of three sales-tax elections. Nothing, not a trace of rail anywhere—although political straining and striving from all the election efforts have set back the agency a bundle in time, money and sullied reputation. By moving purposefully rather than heedlessly ahead, RTD has managed to cover a sizable territory.

The whole-hoggery crowd, possessed with a consuming ardor for everything at once, hasn't mentioned these facts and is unlikely to call attention to them any time soon—certainly not so long as higher sales-tax levies offer the opportunity to snag personal pots of gold. The mere hope of a sales-tax hike yielded GM Marsella a $25,000 cash bonus for "advancing" a tax bill during the 2002 Colorado General Assembly. Should that tax increase actually come to pass, another fortunate few stand to benefit enormously. Hastily planned, quick-fix government projects afford well-placed consultants and investment bankers easy entree into the financial hidey-holes where normal profits get laced with swag.

Multiple Extensions

Like it or not (and Marsella and his hirelings have labored to keep the news under wraps), the MAC has shown itself as the little line that could. "The line to nowhere" is what critics used to call it, but these critics have taken a back-breaking pratfall. The MAC is actually the line to everywhere. Once it went into operation new lines didn't have to start from scratch. They could begin their journeys with a 5.3-mile head start.

• **Southwest Line.** This encompasses 8.7 track miles and 15.8 line miles (miles that can be traveled without changing vehicles). After a raging dispute over which should come first—this or the Southeast Corridor—the board finally decided to go southwest, although creditable evidence indicated the alternative direction might turn out nearly five to ten times more productive. Bureaucratic momentum carried the day, nonetheless. Once the steamrollers started moving westward, there was never a realistic chance of anybody intercepting them.

But despite its second-tier status, the Southwest line has enjoyed runaway popularity, with passenger boardings climbing some 40 percent above forecasts. Unanimously approved by DRCOG the line cost $175 million—$55 million in RTD funds plus a $120 million federal contribution. This federal contribution inadvertently presented US Representatives Dan Schaefer (R, Arapahoe) and Diana DeGette (D, Denver) and US Senator Ben Nighthorse Campbell (R) a temptation they could not resist, namely a chance to pretend that Denver light rail was all their doing. With fine and generous smiles for the voters and lordly little put-downs for the local yokels who crafted the project, Colorado's political royalty latched onto the self-promoting opportunity with nary a hesitation. (The Washington self-esteem machine never turns off.)

Thus do big fish eat little fish and all their progeny, Colorado-style. Thank heaven that at least some federal office holders, notably US Senator Wayne Allard (R), manage to hold their egos reasonably in check even after reaching Washington, aka "The Big Rock Candy Mountain."[12]

• *Platte Valley Line.* Consisting of 1.8 track miles, the line here seamlessly connects with 11.7 miles southwest; and when the Southeast Corridor is completed it will also connect with 22.6 miles southeast. The first line proposed and rammed through by development interests instead of board members, the line cuts off from the MAC just north of the 10th and Osage stop, meandering from there by several sports and entertainment venues: 1) Invesco Field at Mile High, 2) Pepsi Center, 3) Six Flags, 4) Lower Downtown (LoDo), 5) Coors Field.

Initial requests for the Platte Valley line came from Gwen Anderson, Trillium Corporation lobbyist, and Steve Farber, partner in Colorado's primo political law firm of Browstein, Hyatt, Farber and Strickland. As originally laid out to board members, the request called for Valley "stakeholders" (as listed above) to pay for building the 1.8-mile line—with perhaps a small amount from RTD. No more than a very "tiny" contribution is how early Platte Valley booster Denver City Councilwoman Debbie Ortega (District 9) frequently characterized RTD's proposed involvement.

The idea seemed progressive and equitable. Valley stakeholders would win by tying on to what could ultimately become a 100-mile, multi-billion-dollar light-rail system. RTD would benefit by channeling its construction savings into higher and better uses. For example, it could start working on the long-sought DIA connection.

So wouldn't it have been pretty from a public-interest viewpoint if the deal had worked out as originally promised? Yes, indeed, everything would have looked drop-dead gorgeous, except the deal failed to work out as expected. After all the sweet talk was done and reality set in, government picked up the lion's share ($50 million) of the total tab ($52 million), with so-called "shareholders" seeing fit to kick in little more than $2 million.

Worse from RTD's standpoint than even this expensive reversal, Trillum Corporation and its friends at the Metro Denver Chamber of Commerce and Downtown Partnership contrived to unload on RTD as part of the deal the scandalously overpriced, down-at-the-heels $50 million Union Station. How did Trillum Corporation and helpers manage to finagle such a handsome sum? By dreaming up, in collaboration with various board and staff members, the patently false story that RTD absolutely must transform the old train depot into a refurbished light-rail station. Without a huge station, these fabulists insisted, neither the Platte Valley line nor other prospective lines could perform effectively.[13] What mind-boggling claptrap! It is owing to semantic confusion alone that officials figure light rail needs "stations" at all. All light rail really requires is simple "stops."

Another reason the deal slipped so slickly into place: Chairwoman Mary Blue and staff kept major arguments against buying Union Station hidden from public sight—a manipulative disgrace the author follows up on in Chapter 14 where we delve into how RTD's current leadership has unlawfully sequestered time after time over the past several years contrary opinion and unpleasant truths. Chairs Bob Tonsing and Mary Blue have never subscribed to the open-government doctrine that sovereign citizens are entitled to look at all the facts, not just the pretty ones.

Financing the Platte Valley line provided in summation a quick-and-dirty lesson in what old-fashioned door-to-door encyclopedia salesmen used to call "bait-and-switch"—a phrase signifying a living-room shtick wherein the salesman begins his pitch with an absurdly low price and then gradually jacks it up to its intended level. Successful bait-and-switches normally require duplicitous but talented salespeople matched against opportunistic but gullible marks.

• *Southeast Line.* According to many astute observers, this is shaping up as the premier route in the entire system. When completed the line will run 19.6 track miles and 26.7 line miles.

A long and drawn-out tug-of-war preceded board approval—a contest replete with anger, double-dealing, histrionics and more than a little abracadabra foolishness. At one end of the tug-rope, by far the heaviest end, were directors who having committed themselves to building-everything-at-once balked at construction to the southeast. The light end was manned by Director Gloria Holliday and the author, exponents of doing what could be done—which at this moment in time meant moving forward with a single line to the southeast.

Given the enormous disparity in weight, why didn't the all-at-once contestants score an immediate victory? Because they simply could not do what they wanted to do, no matter how vigorously they tried. This stemmed from the fact that the third leg of the stool, the funding leg, couldn't be located and in truth did not exist. They could put the brakes on the southeast line, but they couldn't satisfy their appetite for another four or five lines all at once. Reality wouldn't allow it.

Like snarling and sharp-fanged dogs in the manger, they couldn't consume the fodder themselves but they sure could scare away the milk cows, which is exactly what they proceeded to do for a prolonged period of time. Happily helping the intransigence along, GM Marsella and his palace guard from the RTD development/planning department kept the board in contrived confusion by misrepresenting relevant data, and by blowing technical smoke. Seeking the unattainable nirvana of getting everything immediately, these folks put the much-anticipated Southeast Corridor in considerable danger. Whether they behaved so destructively out of ignorance or spite the author cannot say for certain—although he can attest to instances when several participants came to bear an uncannily strong resemblance to Aesop's demonic dogs.

Trying to build without additional tax revenues "will bankrupt RTD" GM Marsella averred, with his opinion immediately seconded by the sycophantic board majority. He was wrong, emphatically wrong. Marsella and his board majority confessed to error later, although the admission was embodied in their actions, never in so many words. What they finally decided was to go with the Southeast Corridor and to finance it out of current funds. The lopsided infighting took a toll, however. Trust and transparency faded dramatically and matters of significance began refracting through a glass of exclusion and polarization.

• *Denver International Airport Line.* As recounted in Chapter 8, RTD originally planned to construct its first light-rail line north from downtown Denver to Five Points and then east along Martin Luther King Jr. Boulevard to Stapleton Airport. The line could then at some later date be extended all the way to DIA, about 25 total miles. These plans were jettisoned, though, when the board decided it had better forget about trying to bushwhack a trail through unfriendly territory.

But even in the wake of this retreat the board never lost its vision of light rail to DIA, persisting in the dogged belief that a line here held tremendous potential. So it began casting about for a more attractive routing, such as possibly Smith Road, and a more propitious starting time. That time has now arrived or is at least rapidly drawing nigh. More broadly appreciated in 2003 than ever before, with all kinds of citizens regarding it a civic glory, light rail—including most definitely a DIA line—can still be put in place without raising taxes.

Making Everybody Transfer

An insufferable new threat has unfortunately begun to darken the scene. A relatively new consortium—including RTD management—has decided it would like to replace light rail in part with diesel trains. This group would also run its planned DIA diesel line from Union Station rather than from the existing electric terminal at 30th and Downing.[14]

A more ghastly choice cannot be imagined. That this arrangement will take both more track and more money goes almost without saying.[15] Even worse, bordering on the sinister actually, the plan will require virtually every DIA passenger to change trains at Union Station. Equally reprehensible it will decimate stops from which riders can shoot all the way to DIA without transferring. If the line is tied in to 30th and Downing as originally planned, these haunting specters disappear. Most passengers will not need transfers. They can also board through-trains to DIA at some 30 different stops.

As of early 2003 the issue—as outlandish as it appears—still hangs in doubt, but with Big Development holding a monstrous advantage, largely because many ordinary citizens don't understand what's at stake. If the final decision is to proceed with diesel from Union Station, readers can safely assume that Big Development has won—and also that something has gone disastrously wrong inside public-oriented planning.

On the other hand if the decision comes down in favor of light rail from 30th and Downing, riders should hire a dance band and commence with merrymaking. Sensible public transport with an eye toward passenger convenience will have succeeded in both fending off a disaster and racking up a victory.

Governor Bill Owens' Contributions

People change their minds about light-rail for many different reasons. Some sing out with something sounding very like "eureka" the first time they take a ride. Others let themselves be persuaded by operating and financial statistics. Still others succumb to peer and political pressures. But while it's easy to list general reasons for change, attributing concrete motives to specific individuals seems far dicier. It's virtually impossible, for instance, to say exactly why Governor Bill Owens reversed his position. All that's known with certainty: He has indeed executed an about-face.

During the late 1980s and early 1990s, you couldn't find a more dedicated light-rail enemy than then-State Senator Bill Owens. He rejoiced in taking a chainsaw to it at every opportunity. Further, by pushing Senate Bill 208 in 1991 he did as much as any member of the state legislature to tear the MAC to shreds. As discussed in Chapter 3, this bill was the weapon that very nearly deconstructed light rail before citizens had a chance to evaluate a proper demonstration.

But, lo and behold, while campaigning for governor during 1998 Owens executed an amazing turnaround. He began favoring the idea of constructing a single light-rail line, the line running along the Southeast Corridor. Upon becoming governor Owens integrated plans for this line into his program for widening I-25 from six to ten lanes.

Several years later during the 2002 legislative session, the governor took his new posture to the outer limit. He threw his support (the sine qua non of passage) behind Senate Bill 179, which, although thinly veiled by political gloss, gives RTD an open sesame to ask voters for a 0.4 percentage-point sales-tax hike. Should the question ultimately pass, RTD will finally come into the greatly enlarged cash flow for which so many people have hankered—partly because they don't fully fathom alternative financing.

Without Governor Owens' advice and consent RTD probably would not be constructing the Southeast line. Almost certainly it would not be out hustling voters for a big sales-tax boost. Whether this is what the governor consciously intended, appearances point to his conversion over the years from fervid antagonist to faithful partisan.

Notes

1. *The Trolley Song, Meet Me in St. Louis*, Metro-Goldwyn-Mayer, 1944.
2. *Make no little plans: they have no magic to stir men's blood.* Daniel H. Burnham, early 20th century Chicago architect, *New York Review of Books*, March 28, 2002, p. 2002.
3. Marginal cost is the additional cost that a producer incurs by making one additional unit of output. Present value is the value today of a future stream of payments (benefits) discounted at the prevailing (discount) interest rate.
4. The sun was later removed under the leadership of publicist Scott Read and GM Peter Cipolla (who preceded GM Marsella) and also some of the same folks who obliterated the name "MAC," replacing it with "Central Corridor."
5. Jack McCroskey, "MAC On The Move," *Rocky Mountain News*, Denver; 5 July 1992. "A frequently reprinted report written in 1989 for the US Department of Transportation has generated all manner of hostility and bias toward light rail. Committing sins of both omission and commission, the report omits all reference to the monumental government subsidies going to petroleum-powered vehicles. Further, it doesn't include in its overall conclusion the results from hugely successful light-rail systems such as the one in San Diego."
6. Larry McMurtry, *Lonesome Dove*, NY; Simon & Schuster, 1985.
7. Patricia Nelson Limerick, *Something In Its Soil*, NY; W. W. Norton, 2000.
8. Philip Morris' first Marlboro Man, Charles, died of lung cancer from cigarettes, Tara Parker Pope (2002). First US Surgeon General Report on smoking was issued in 1964, first cigarette package warning in 1966. Nazi Germany actually led the world by several decades in cigarette research and control. German cigarette consumption fell by more than half from 1940 to 1950. See *The Nazi War on Cancer*, Robert N. Proctor, 1999, p.244.
9. US Surgeon General's Report, 2001.
10. Many Americans laugh it off whenever charges of conspicuous consumption are leveled against them—and in truth conspic-

uous consumption if a crime at all is victimless. Trying to impress one's neighbors with material goods may seem a trifle tacky, but it is not in the same awful league as berating one's neighbors or insulting them or playing heavy-metal music through overpowered speakers. Even Thorstein Veblen would have agreed.

11. Absent a general theory concerning whether it's easier to stop smoking or driving, please permit the author a personal anecdote. As a young person, he both smoked and drove to wild excess. He now does neither—and hasn't for 30 years. Giving up driving was far easier than giving up cigarettes. A car is only a car, after all, but a cigarette is a smoke.

12. To his everlasting credit Allard hasn't played pathetic little games. He's demonstrated a largesse of spirit that enables him to acknowledge the contributions of others, even those who are far from his political equals.

13. Speaking at length and in honeyed tones, members of the RTD bureaucracy and board paint grandiose pictures of RTD making a fortune in real-estate profits by turning Union Station into a modern marvel of commercial hustle and retail bustle. Unfortunately (and unethically), Chairwoman Mary Blue wouldn't allow open discussion of what happened when the elected board let staff get caught up in similar illusions during the early 1970s. At that time RTD invested many millions in what was then called the Galbreath Building. Over the quarter-century since then, RTD has lost a million or so every year, for a total of $25 to $50 million (depending on how it's calculated). Today, almost nobody remembers that the big brown building sitting on the uptown end of the 16th Street Mall with the big blue DENVER POST sign on its façade belongs to RTD and costs taxpayers ever more with each passing day. For information on these losses, see two audits closely held within RTD's files: 1) *An Evaluation of the Return on Investment From Civic Center Air Rights Lease*, Leventhal & Horwith, Denver, 18 August 1986; 2) *Report of the Internal Auditor, Review of Galbreath Air Rights Lease*, General Manager Office, Denver, 12 April 1985.

14. Denver Mayor Wellington Webb is an outspoken proponent of the DIA line from Union Station. Why? The author does not know for certain, but isn't convinced the reason has much to do with better public transport.

15. DRCOG's staff presented reports during the "Guide the Ride" political contest showing that heavy rail from Union Station to DIA would cost less than light rail from 30th and Downing. They did so by using the obvious trick of calculating costs for a single line of heavy rail, and a double line of light rail. Light rail would definitely cost less-plus it would avoid diesel fumes. It is sad but true: DRCOG will, like so many others, say virtually anything to win its point. RTD's staff swallowed DRCOG's presentation without visible qualms or audible protest.

12

REVEREND MALTHUS
CONSIDERS CONGESTION

F.A. Hayek, Milton Friedman and Adam Smith
Look at Subsidies

Reviled by his contemporaries as a mean-spirited spoilsport who hated little children and portrayed by later generations as a false prophet of disaster, the Reverend Thomas Malthus was in actuality neither of these things. In real life he comported himself with the open-hearted benevolence befitting a gentle and genteel Anglican minister *cum* economist.[1]

At the same time Malthus had a mind of his own plus the firmness of backbone needed to break ranks with his peers when he thought them mistaken. This he did, sharply and audaciously, on the question of imminent utopia—a topic that stimulated passionate debate during the 18th-century Age of Enlightenment.

Public philosophers, many at least, believed they had uncovered the underlying nature and instrumental use of human reason. Further they thought that by using their discoveries as a blueprint for the future they could construct in very short order a practical Paradise here on earth—a place where social and economic distress would quickly evaporate. These ideas reached their fullest flower in the Marquis de Condorcet's profoundly credulous *History of Justice* (1774)[2] and William Godwin's *Inquiry Concerning Political Justice* (1793).[3] Condorcet proclaimed, with Godwin's concurrence: The world will soon attain universal virtue and happiness. Material shortages will disappear, and life will extend without limit. (Which while not exactly immortality seems disturbingly similar.)

Trouble in Paradise

Unable to bear such conjectures in silence, Malthus challenged them out loud and head-on. Not so fast, he argued, the world isn't as malleable as all that. Consider the stumbling block of rapidly growing population *vis-a-vis* more slowly growing agricultural output. He then spelled out the logical consequence of these not unreasonable assumptions in his *Essay on Population* (1778).[4]

Because of natural sexual proclivities, Malthus observed, population over time tends to expand geometrically (1,2,4,8,16), whereas agricultural output, because of pressures to plant diminishingly productive land, tends to expand only arithmetically (1,2,3,4,5).

If and when the trends intersect, the Grim Reaper takes charge. His job is to mop up marginal lives, using an array of pathologies—most commonly famine, plague, war. Malthus' bluntly uncomfortable point: In one way or another when population outstrips the means to feed it, population will necessarily be reduced. Wishful thinking about living happily ever after (much less living forever) will be soundly dashed.

Sometimes the terrors pass swiftly. At other times they drag on and on, with superfluous people huddling together like so many prisoner chickens subsisting on a thin gruel down the gullet. Ultimately this poor fare vanishes, too.

The scene Malthus projected was repugnant and maddening. So much so it sent those with utopian impulses into a blinding rage; those with more moderate feelings of optimism it merely infuriated. No wonder many of Malthus' contemporaries, along with commentators down through the years, often forgot that in his later demographic work, *Second Essay on Population* (1798), he began delving into positive ways of escaping what came to be called the "Malthusian Nightmare."[5] Malthus' chief preventative check to overpopulation and catastrophe? "Moral restraint"—that is, the chaste postponement of .marriage and the resulting diminishment in births.[6]

Problems and Principles

The inevitable question: What's all this got to do with urban mobility? Surprisingly enough and despite the wide gulf between them, human famine and traffic congestion share conceptual similarities.[7] They've both been brought center stage by seemingly inexorable trends—negative tendencies that can't be wished away but must be corrected, in so far as correctives are possible, through human thought and effort.

Short of a successful seance (altogether improbable), there's really no way to sit down for coffee and a chat with the good Reverend Malthus about current developments. What we can do, based on the problems and principles he set forth, is use his classic analysis of overpopulation to help sketch the problems associated with gridlock.

- **One.** The problem isn't because, as short-story writer Flannery O'Connor's famous title had it, *All Things That Rise Must Converge.*[8] The problem lies in *differential* growth rates, in the fact that some things grow faster than others—as, for example, during Malthus' time Great Britain's population apparently climbed more rapidly than the means to sustain it.

- **Two.** From Malthus' viewpoint population as determined by births constitutes the key variable—although it's crystal clear today (and wasn't completely unknown during Malthus' time) large numbers of secondary variables also affect outcomes. Lengthening life spans raise the demand side, for example. Improvements in agricultural productivity and distribution boost supply.

- **Three.** Most crucially if the demand for, say, food outstrips supply for any appreciable length of time, then prices will rise to levels where some would-be customers are forced to do without. From this moment onward, if the tendencies continue, population will oscillate around subsistence. Much the same holds true for other commodities, housing, clothing, medical care and so on. Where the demand for these rises faster than the supply for extended periods some consumers will be forced from the marketplace.

"Every Day in Every Way"

Had the tendencies worked themselves out the way Malthus' original calculus suggests, today's United States would look like an utterly different country. More like a dreary wasteland than like the fulfillment of the supremely optimistic forecast made during the 1920s by philosopher Emile Coué: "Every day in every way, we're getting better and better."

Despite almost doubling their numbers over the past half-century—150 million in 1950 versus 275 million in 2000 — Americans aren't just better off (speaking mainly of material goods and services), they have become *immensely* better off. Indeed, it's hard to find statistical yardsticks that deny this cheerful conclusion. Virtually every observable measure indicates 50 or more years of substantial gains.

Broad and long, the winner's list deserves reiteration: personal income, health, housing, education, leisure, science, communication, poverty reduction, plus the compassionate care of young and old. Most contemporary Americans, it appears, are ready to acknowledge these spectacular accomplishments although just a few decades ago they seemed reluctant to do so. Why the change in outlook? Why the emerging desire to glory and even revel in good fortune?

A partial explanation may derive from the simple passage of time since the 1930's Great Depression, a catastrophic collapse that gradually assumed the status of heart-pounding bugaboo. Until very recently depression fears appeared always poised to rattle in the night at the first scent of business slippage.[9]

Another explanation rests on the sterling work undertaken

by economist/statisticians Julian Simon and Ben Wattenberg, both of whom have devoted considerable portions of their professional careers to delivering the upbeat message. With strict honesty and eschewing the usual purple prose, both Wattenburg's *The Good News Is the Bad News Is Wrong* (1984)[10] and Simon's *It's Getting Better All the Time* (2000)[11] chart the trends with uncommon sense and admirable directness.

Glaring Omission

Even so and as skillfully as the broad picture is rendered, it doesn't take a seasoned critic to detect places where the canvas shows through.[12] The most important blemish from this volume's standpoint is traffic congestion. Congestion isn't improving, it's growing worse. A lot worse.

During the three decades beginning in 1970, the number of vehicle-miles driven in the United States skyrocketed some 130 percent; during the same time period lane-miles rose only 15 percent.[13] Putting these data into a Malthusian framework lane-miles (population) grew almost nine times faster than road-lane capacity (food production). Had this variance occurred in the relation between population and food, then in accord with Malthusian principles Americans wouldn't be battling obesity today.[14] They would be struggling to overcome hunger and starvation.

Given such disparate growth rates no one should be surprised it's taking commuters longer and longer to travel to and from work, with the average commute climbing to 24.3 minutes in 2000, up about three minutes from 1960. Widely perceived and excruciatingly felt, these aggravations need little elaboration. Almost everybody has experienced them, whether commuting or going to the grocery store or just heading out to a fast-food joint. It's no fun sitting inside a boxed-in automobile in a slow-moving traffic jam.

The important questions facing the community today is how to alleviate the pain. Malthusian logic suggests two immediate answers. One, reduce the number of trips—in other words cut back on the American desire to move around. Two, increase *proportionately* the number of lane-miles. But as logical as these responses may sound they strike this observer as highly implausible.

- **Less Moving Around.** Among the most popular notions about how to contain automobile trips: 1) Curbing population growth; 2) Living over the store or moving closer to one's job; 3) Working at home.

   Possibilities no doubt, and the author endorses each of them to one degree or another. But they also come with cat-cradle problems, the first being that they conflict with other community goals.[15]

   Plus there is no way to control such variables through public policy. Policies may nudge them one way or another, and such nurturing may or may not supplement private efforts, depending on individual sentiments. But there is little likelihood that public-policy changes with regard to these essentially private decisions will substantially reduce congestion.

- **Build Streets and Roads Proportionately.** Simply not possible. Just to catch up with miles-driven growth rates during the past few decades, the space given over to Denver streets and roads would have to increase some nine times. Should a land-eating orgy such as this actually take place, Denver would wind up without enough room left over for a small statue of Henry Ford or enough greenery for a medium-sized Caesar salad.

   Clairvoyance isn't required; only basic arithmetic and geography are needed to see that definite limits exist on how much space can be devoted to urban roads and streets. Asphalt dealers and contractors aren't apt to be put out of business any time soon, but neither should they be allowed to pave over entire urban areas.

Technology is the Answer

Except for the world's poorest countries where mass starvation occurs even today with alarming frequency, food production at the beginning of the 21st century is keeping abreast of population growth. This continuing gap between the food and population curves, with the food curve on top, results very largely from productivity gains—from better seeds producing more prolific plants yielding more crops per acre. The Green Revolution, as some call it, not only fits Reverend Malthus' model, it points the way toward successful traffic-congestion management.

Scientific traffic control can promote the more efficient use of finite urban space, just as fertilizers, pesticides and herbicides can increase per-acre agricultural yields. But these techniques are notably circumscribed. Over the long haul, agriculture has scored its major gains by planting improved seeds that in turn produce more productive plants. Similarly urban transportation in the future will be forced to employ more productive vehicles—vehicles carrying more passengers. The reality of trying to expand lane-miles in proportion to the number of trips is that it cannot be done, and hence will not be done. (Which it is not to say that a handful of asphalt-besotted oddballs may not try.)

Vehicles satisfying the requirement for greater passenger capacity need not be invented, they need only be reclaimed (see Chapter 3). These are Frank Sprague's trolleys reborn. Now called "light rail," they fit the bill in virtually every respect. Larger and more powerful, speeded up and quieted down, full of daylight and totally free of odoriferous emissions, these machines are many times more capacious than anything on city streets today:

• One light-rail car can transport about 160 passengers. Compare this to about 40 passengers per standard public-transport bus, and just a little more than one passenger per average private automobile.

- Because RTD's light-rail trains usually consist of three cars during peak hours, the ratio during the region's heaviest traffic figures at 480 to 40 to 1.

These ratios seem as dazzling in their own way as the difference between early American ears of corn (about two inches long) and modern ears (about 13 inches long).

Government Subsidies

Automobiles and light rail depend very substantially on government subsidies—federal, state and local. There is no reason to think these subsidies will end any time soon. So which gets the most, automobiles or rail? The answer, confoundingly enough, depends on who you talk to. Some say automobiles, some say rail. And each side vouches for its answer with impressive-looking, statistics-laden studies.

What's the reason for the continuing dichotomy? The answers aren't testable by experiment or observation. Falling outside scientific methodology, they cannot be falsified. This is because they are based on normative rather than positive grounds.

For example, if one elects to include the costs to the United States of protecting Middle Eastern oil, by far the heaviest subsidies will be seen as flowing to automobiles. On the other hand, if one excludes these expenditures, the response slants back toward public transport. Unless of course the community's loss of property taxes on the space it devotes to streets and roads are included, which will warp the answer back in the opposite direction. And so it goes, on and on, without ever coming even close to a definitive conclusion.

Thus, although the author leans toward including all secondary costs, including a goodly chunk of the expenditures required to ensure continuing access to cheap oil, he is unable to demonstrate this preference in an entirely objective way. Nor can he or anyone else do so in a manner that will convince all parties to the debate.

Hayek, Friedman and Smith

Other popular and pertinent questions: Is it a good idea to subsidize urban transportation? Does it make for good policy in the United States today?

The questions seem more socially charged today than a few decades ago, largely because of the burgeoning influence of free-market philosophers. Reinvigorated by Frederick A. Hayek with his *Road to Serfdom* (1944)[15] and led on to remarkable triumphs by economist Milton Friedman with *Capitalism and Freedom* (1962) and many other writings, free-market economic and political philosophies comprise what is possibly the most important intellectual movement in the United States during the 20th century's second half.

Hayek would give such subsidies a pass, according to his quite direct statements. In commenting, for example, on what economists call "externalities," he wrote:[16]

> In many instances there is a divergence between the items which enter into private calculation and those which affect social welfare; and, when this divergence becomes important, some method under other than the competitive markets may have to be found to supply the services in question. Thus neither the provision of sign posts on the roads, nor in most circumstances, that of the roads themselves can be paid for by every individual user.[17]

Friedman's take on the specific issue of subsidies to public transport is fuzzier. He may slip an approval in under his free-market rubric, but then again he may not. Only one point here stands indisputable: If subsidies there must be, then Friedman finds those provided at local levels far preferable to those deriving from either state or federal sources.[18]

Along these same lines, it will be worthwhile to inquire into the opinions of Adam Smith, the father of free-market economics.

Perhaps the first thing to note about Smith's writings is that his timeless metaphor "invisible hand" is exactly that: a metaphor. It is not a detailed description of the market mechanism, nor is it an exposition of how the pursuit of private welfare working through unfettered markets redounds to public advantage. Neither, most emphatically, should it be interpreted as a retreat into mysticism.

Understanding the towering benefits of free markets, Smith loathed encumbrances that destroy them: Feudalism, mercantilism and price-fixing, whether by government fiat or private connivance.[19] But while he set great store in economic self-interest working through free markets to handle most economic transactions, Smith never mistook these markets for the Will of God (as do many doctrinaire Libertarians).

He used the phrase "invisible hand" but twice in his 590-page *Wealth of Nations* (1776) and not at all in his almost equally instructive *Theory of Moral Sentiments* (1759).[20] Nor did he show himself by any means inimical to civil society, specifically supporting government efforts to reduce poverty, educate children and provide certain kinds of public infrastructure such as roads. All and all, one finds scant reason to think that Smith would, were he alive today, consider subsidies to public transport destructively inconsistent with free-market economics. And there's no cause whatsoever to think he would automatically prefer automobile subsidies over those devoted to light rail.

Holding the Line on Costs

Moving from the private to the public sector changes institutions in profound and unsettling ways. The most important is that the shift enables these institutions to evade various market imperatives. For example:

In private markets firms that waste resources go out of business—not overnight necessarily but sooner or later. Governments that waste resources, on the other hand, can stay in business practically forever. The reason: While the invisible hand can discipline private firms quite severely, it is in no position to say "boo" to government enterprises.

In the best of all possible worlds, this exemption might encourage government enterprises to try extra hard to avoid waste. Sadly, in practice these outfits usually head off in the opposite direction, following the path of least resistance. It's the lack of market discipline, most commonly, that leads governments down the garden path into managerial carelessness and sloth—and into the boggy sinkhole in which RTD now sits.

Among the many examples that one might use to illustrate the point, questionable contracting hits the author as especially exasperating. Government contracting reaches its most irresponsible level when pitting taxpayer money on one side of the table against empty boxes on the other. As troubling as it is to watch high-ranking government officials making cozy with outside vendors and contractors, what really shoots the eyebrows is seeing these officials steer major-money deals toward acquaintances (perhaps cronies) who in a hard-nosed economic sense wholly lack credentials.

Intervening in normal purchasing-department practices, GM Marsella insisted on awarding an $11.4 million bus-manufacturing contract (plus options for much more) on 1 April 1995 to acquaintances who called themselves "Columbine Inc." The most arresting feature this ghostly entity presented was the gaping hole where its bona fides should have been. Columbine Inc. had neither past nor present. It had no track record in producing buses, no manufacturing facilities, no operating equipment, no employees, no money in the bank, no long-term capital in the offing. The company's first tangible asset was *ex post facto*, spinning into existence after RTD inked the contract and consisting of the contract itself.

Would Columbine, Inc. adhere to its agreements? Could it deliver? A taxpayer-owned entity like RTD should never have had to ask such questions. Not when there were plenty of financially responsible manufacturers around who would perform as promised. The risk was altogether unnecessary. It represented a losing poker game played with taxpayer money.

But the answer to the question is yes, Columbine delivered—in a thoroughly compromised kind of way. The promised vehicles when they finally arrived were more than two years late. They quickly and deservedly gained a reputation for unreliability. RTD mechanics have had to undertake repairs that manufacturer's warranties should have covered. The company's ability to live up to its guarantee obligations seems problematic. And despite many solemn pledges to the contrary, the vehicles came in onerously overpriced. Twenty-six with an originally agreed upon price of $375,000 each ultimately cost $586,000 each. This over-charge alone amounts to $5.4 million or more than 50 percent. (In the interim the company changed its name to Transportation Technique L.L.C.)

Privatization

In the same vein, shoddy contracting has slopped over into various other areas—such as bus-route privatization. An ungainly and misleading term, "privatization" in the United States signifies mainly hiring private business firms to produce public goods and services.[21] Under privatization arrangements at RTD, the board supposedly retains control over both the quantity and quality of bus service, including fares, frequency, and stops, plus other items falling within the scope of service.

Propelling the drive for privatization is the belief that it saves money, and enables RTD to offer essentially the same service at lower costs.[21] For this reason the Colorado General Assembly required RTD to try out the concept on 20 percent (since raised to 35 percent) of its bus-route mileage with Senate Bill 164 (1988). An ensuing study by KPMG-Peat Mitchell, a national accounting and consulting firm, claimed RTD realized a roughly 40 percent saving on its privatized routes during the late 1980s and early '90s.[22]

But since this study the wheels under bus-route privatization have begun falling off. Privatization seeks savings, but the goal has been imprudently betrayed by the very officials entrusted to implement it.

With the advent of the Marsella regime numerous unqualified companies have been hired to do the job:

• A politically well-connected law firm has been allowed to nose into the contracting process. It pulled all the proper strings for one firm that later marooned hundreds of disabled patrons, some of them gravely ill.

• Other dodgy deals have left passengers by the thousands stranded by the road forlorn and alone, and more than likely wishing they had done the driving themselves instead of taking the bus.

• In order to keep service cobbled together, RTD has had to spend many millions to bail out failing providers, and to clean up some of the messier consequences flowing from its improper actions.

The total cost of these and similar blunders is a question shrouded in mystery. Dollar losses have not been calculated and probably won't be so long as RTD's patchy bookkeeping entombs some accounts and fiddles others. But it's no big stretch to surmise that the managerial misadventures surrounding privatization have eaten up most theoretical savings. One further effect stemming from this mismanagement is that it projects RTD as an overstuffed ATM that's incapable of distinguishing valid from invalid withdrawals—a crazy premise, of course, but a thought that exacerbates what is already a large problem: too much managerial waste, too little board oversight. Another bad effect: It encourages the cover-up and perpetuation of numerous curious and worrisome administrative practices.

One of RTD's most pressing priorities should be to wipe away these wicked stains. Exposing itself to the democratic blessings of open discussion and free speech would make for an excellent start. No institution run by mere mortals should go without constant analysis and criticism.

Notes

1. Contemporaries William Cobbett and Robert Southey loathed Malthus. The first told him, "I have, during my life, detested many men, but never anyone so much as you." The latter said, "It is my heart's desire to put his rascally book to death and damnation." But financier and classical economist David Ricardo, who knew Malthus intimately and debated economic issues with him for almost 50 years, said, "He's the grandest, most generous and amiable person I have known."

2. Marquis de Condorcet, "History of Justice," Argo A. O'Connor, F. M. Condorcet, J. Johnson, eds., *Oeuvres*, London; 1803.

3. Godwin was the father of Mary Shelley, novelist, poet and critic of lasting influence, who wrote the classic *Frankenstein*.

4. T.R. Malthus, *An Essay on Population*, London; NY; Dent; Dutton, [c 1958]

5. E.A. Wrigley, David Saunder, eds., "Second Essay on Population," *Works of Thomas Robert Malthus*, London; Pickering Press, 1986.

6. An Anglican minister of his place and time, Malthus opposed birth control and abortion.

7. That the similarities are conceptual rather than flesh and blood deserves repeating. However awful gridlock and road rage, they don't hold a candle to the sunken bellies and slow deaths of famine. It is character-building, perhaps, to remind ourselves of these important differences.

8. Flannery O'Connor, *All Things That Rise Must Converge*, NY; Farrar, Straus and Giroux, 1965.

9. The effects of deep trauma can apparently go on and on even across decades and generations. Although the Great Depression no longer impinges as directly as it once did on American attitudes, there's no doubt its effects linger still. Nor is this in any way unique. John Keegan in his *First World War* (2001) reports that the sacrificial Battle of the Somme, July-November 1916 "marked the end of an age of vital optimism in British life that has never been recovered." Dick Russell, in *Eye of the Whale* (2001) tells the story of the Pacific Ocean's gray whale. Only many decades after the commercial slaughter

of the species had completely stopped did these gentle leviathans drop their aggressive behavior toward occupied boats.

10. Ben J. Wattenberg, *The Good News Is The Bad News Is Wrong*, NY; Simon and Schuster, 1984

11. Stephen Moore, Julian Lincoln Simon, *It's Getting Better All The Time: 100 Greatest Trends of the Last 100 Years*, Washington, D.C.; Cato Institute, 2000

12. Omissions of growing concern especially since 9/11/01, are mounting social and economic inequities worldwide. In 1960 the world's richest countries enjoyed a per capita Gross Domestic Product (GDP) 18 times greater than the world's 20 poorest countries. In 2000 the rich countries GDP stood 37 times higher. World Bank data show that more than a billion people around the globe exist on less than $1 a day.

13. Fueling these increases are a 32 percent gain in population; 63 percent in number of drivers; 90 percent in number of vehicles. *American Highway Users Alliances.*

14. Surgeon General reports that most American adults—more than 60 percent—are overweight with the obesity rate increasing in every state and among all racial and ethnic groups. The alarming statistics result primarily from careless eating combined with negligible exercise. For specifics on one cause see: *Fast Food Nation: The Dark Side of the All American Meal*, Schlosser, Eric, Boston; Houghton-Mifflin, 2001.

15. Slower population growth bumps up against opposition to severely restricted immigration. Living over-the-store conflicts with desires for detached homes and large yards. Working at home interferes with the creative marketplace.

16. Externalities are the discrepancies between private and social costs, or between private and social benefits. The key aspect of externalities is interdependence without compensation. The existence of externalities provides a strong argument for government intervention in the private economy.

17. F. A. Hayek, *The Road to Serfdom*, Chicago, University of Chicago Press, 1944.

18. Milton Friedman, *Capitalism and Freedom*, Chicago; University of Chicago Press, 1962. Friedman's most profound and useful

contribution to economic understanding and practice is, in the author's opinion, his magnificent *Monetary History of the United States: 1867-1960*, Friedman, Milton and Schwartz, Jacobson Anna, Princeton; Princeton University Press, 1963.

19. Adam Smith, *Wealth of Nations*, Knopf; Distributed by Random House, 1991, 1910.

20. Adam Smith, *The Theory of Moral Sentiments*, Oxford [Oxfordshire]: New York: Clarendon Press, Oxford University Press, 1976.

21. In Europe and Russia, "privatization" means the sale of public facilities to private individuals and corporations.

22. *Denver RTD Privatization Performance Update*, KPMG-Peat Mitchell, 1 November 1991. Held in RTD files.

13

EVERYBODY LOVES A WINNER
Giving Credit Where Credit Is Due

Success or failure?

Conventional ways of evaluating light-rail systems—operating statistics and user testimonials—paint a picture limned with success. Ridership numbers are large and flourishing, both absolutely and compared to initial forecasts. Not only does the verbal roses-to-brickbats ratio stand tall, but many complaints sound like backhanded compliments. "There isn't enough of it," for instance. Or "We need more parking space."

There are also ways of gauging how the public feels about the incremental approach—the techniques RTD employed in getting light rail under way. District voters decisively defeated all-or-nothing proposals (see Chapter 9), but they approved the one-line-at-a-time, debt-increase proposition set before them on 7 November 1999 by a whopping 67 to 33 percent. This constitutes the most flattering outcome in RTD's electoral history.

There's yet another way of weighing public attitudes. Smacking just a little of one-upmanship and thereby maybe a shade suspect, the method serves nonetheless as an edifying yardstick. It surveys public figures who during the daunting start-up years either slammed the idea or washed their hands of it. When Doubting Thomases such as these reverse themselves—not just approving what's gone before but actually taking credit for it—one can confidently conclude that ordinary voters relish the project. *Really* relish it.

Consider some of the more significant reversals:

• **Denver Metro Chamber of Commerce.** A long-time adversary and critic of RTD's elected board of directors, the Metro Chamber fought incremental buildouts of both the MAC and the Southeast Corridor. Battled them until it became obvious that these undertakings would proceed either with or without chamber approbation.

But once the MAC had come into its own the Metro Chamber proclaimed a great victory and showered itself with compliments for a job well done. The same with the Southeast Corridor. After the debt-increase issue was safely on the ballot, owing to the thought and toil of RTD board members, the chamber not only took its customary bows but staked out a quit-claim deed to ownership. With hubris only the swaggering elite dare display, the Metro Chamber crowd not only claimed full credit for electoral victory but began acting as if it had invented the very idea of incrementalism.

Monumentally mistaken on both counts, the Metro Chamber had no business soliciting accolades—not when all it had really done was push on a swinging door. For this service you don't deserve even a miserly tip.

• **Denver Moves.** Question: What's the difference between a rooster that believes its crowing makes the morning sun come up and a campaign committee that thinks it alone decides the winning side in light-rail elections? Answer: The rooster is a bird.

In other salient respects the bird and Denver Moves, a Metro Chamber political front, look a whole lot alike. Both are vivified by outsized egos; both are wedded to the logical fallacy *post hoc propter hoc*; both are flat-out wrong. The world would keep right on turning without the rooster. The ballot question on Southeast Corridor funding would have passed by a huge margin absent the committee.

Denver Moves' easily refutable claims to the contrary reflect the Metro Chamber's determination to take bows for other people's efforts—a callous banditry that diminishes the thief and dishonors his victims, victims the Chamber in an oafish put-down trashed as too grubby and gauche to qualify for membership in haughtily pretentious Denver Moves. George Orwell, who deeply disdained both caste and class, would have savored the hypocrisy.

Come to think of it, there's another important difference between rooster and committee: The bird possesses considerably more class.

• *General Manager Cal Marsella.* Entrepreneurial bureaucrat with a fever for self-promotion, who treats the truth like a wad of Silly Putty that can bounce any old way but straight up. Keep these characterizations in mind when contemplating the Marsella reign. While well below par in overall performance, the man has finessed for himself the highest salary and perks in RTD history. Not just the highest ever, but the highest relative to RTD's rank-and-file.[1] In addition to his $205,000 annual salary Marsella receives yearly cash bonuses *and* deferred compensation. Plus he quadruple-dips into RTD pension programs.

GM Marsella played no part at all in orchestrating the MAC, residing out of state at the time. Further, at every opportunity he undercut plans for building the Southeast Corridor incrementally. He contended first that government revenues were sinking when they were actually shooting through the roof. Later he erroneously insisted that building the Southeast Corridor without tax hikes would put RTD on downhill skids to bankruptcy.

Marsella nonetheless now boasts of having launched Denver light rail and of having secured Southeast Corridor funding—dishonest braggadocio that for inappropriate reasons does the man no harm with the Metro Chamber or in the daily press. At the same time he displays a piratical fondness for tarring those whose contributions to Denver public transport are incomparably greater than his own.

• **New Board Members.** Anyone who has spent time with adolescents en masse knows that many young people believe the world began about the time they first saw day-light. By early adulthood, however, the vast majority have outgrown their illusions. This change not only allows parents and offspring to enjoy an *entante cordiale* before death do they part, it contributes to intergenerational transfers of cultural capital.

RTD hasn't enjoyed equally good fortune during the past few years. Most incoming directors haven't filled their historical lacuna, cavalierly assuming that nothing important happened before they arrived center stage. Oh, they've heard and repeated horror stories about RTD's bad old days but they haven't a glimmer of the progress and breakthroughs that preceded them. This historical gap unlocks a Pandora's Box.

Among other things it leaves the board and hence the public interest more than usually vulnerable to wily real estate operatives and unscrupulous bureaucrats. What's more, it lets board members such as Bill Elfenbein (A) deliberately mislead the electorate. Using telephone calls by the thousands Elfenbein encourages listeners to suppose that he personally brought light rail to pass when in truth he had nothing whatsoever to do with it. It allows Directors Mary Blue (I), and Dick McLean (O) to camouflage their early opposition to the Southeast Corridor as long-term support.

• **Denver Post.** Bob Ewegen, who conceives and writes the paper's RTD editorials, frequently savaged RTD's elected board, attributing to it inadequacies of stunning scope and depth. Then, with an unexplained change of heart, the flogging stopped. Later he began offering up praise for elected boards, saying they're better than other forms of governance—although his encomiums often sound more than a little forced.

For a long while Ewegen also expressed distaste for the idea of building the Southeast Corridor incrementally. As soon as the project took on done-deal status, however, he bestowed upon it his redundant approval. Today the *Post* exalts those who fought against the incremental concept, acting for all the world as if the enemies of step-by-step buildouts such as GM Marsella were in fact its progenitors. The distortion here is nothing less than grotesque.

With so many reversals under his extravagantly generous belt, Ewegen might have gained renown for his well-practiced trick of colliding with himself in mid-somersault. He hasn't—partly because newspapers seldom acknowledge their own flip-flops. The man deserves notoriety even so. He's earned it . . . for his journalistic bullying and bilious broadsides, and for fatuously appointing himself master of the economico-politico universe.

• **Rocky Mountain News.** At the outset of serious strategizing about a possible demonstration line (1989-90), Vincent Carroll, the *News*' editor of the editorial pages, stood in the front ranks of Light-Rail-Haters-United. He began backing off his rigid mind-set after the MAC opened. Sometime after that he began sidling toward support of an incremental buildout along the Southeast Corridor.

Now, probably at ex-publisher Larry Strutton's urging, he embraces the one-line-at-a-time philosophy as if he had discovered the concept—a shift abundantly testified to by various latter-day editorials. Like more than a few pundits, Carroll is prone to mistaking exposition for invention, advocacy for execution.

The late Gene Amole, who was Denver's most influential columnist, proved the exception to the rule that all roads to light rail lead from disfavor to favor. He enthusiastically endorsed plans for the short 1.7-mile MAC line from downtown Denver to 30th and Downing, saying, "It's time we kicked the tires and drove it around the block."[2] But shortly thereafter Amole stoutly rejected extending the MAC from Auraria campus to I-25 and Broadway, although the short MAC line would have doubtlessly backfired, not just failing but failing in a way that would have seriously impinged on future efforts. Why the sharp turnaround? It's hard to say. One guess: He felt, quite simply, that things were going to turn out badly. Another guess: The board's relentless optimism set his nerves on edge.

• **Boulder Daily Camera.** Director Bill Womack (I) and the author met with *Camera* editors fairly early in the game to solicit their MAC endorsement. Apparently mistaking us for Laurel and Hardy, they snickered and laughed and sent us on our way with the feeling that we might find careers as nightclub comics.

Since then, Boulder has become hotter than the hottest jalapeño for light-rail expansion.

• **Denver Councilwomen.** Sharks do it, reporters do it, even the birds and the bees do it. And under the right circumstances maybe every living creature on earth will do it: lose themselves in feeding frenzies.

Elected officials and other political figures certainly forget themselves whenever they spot the slightest chance of hitching their wagons to a wildly popular government program. Such opportunities are rare, of course, largely because highly popular programs are few and far between. Light rail may be Denver's first since . . . well, since we can't remember when.

It's no surprise therefore that many state-and-local political figures now try (via speeches, radio announcements, brochures, etc.) to latch onto a piece of light-rail action—even though the great majority either shunned the original buildout or else attempted to scuttle it. Denver City Councilwomen Joyce Foster (District 4) and Kathleen MacKenzie (District 7) snatch and grab with an abandon that warrants public posting. These two deport themselves in ways that make the old boarding-house reach look demurely graceful. Talk about lack of charm . . . no, wait, talk about crude and callow instead.

Genuine Puzzle

All of which demonstrates rather conclusively that the local power-elite decided somewhere along the line to hijack popular credit for Denver light rail. The question left open is why?

A genuine puzzle, the situation needs consideration (a conclusion being probably impossible) from several angles. To begin at the bottom, why do some top-level bureaucrats, many of whom certainly know better, tag along with Metro Chamber mythology? Consider as a living example RTD publicist Scott Reed—for him "money" seems as good a supposition as any. Making about $130,000 annually (salary plus benefits), Reed takes home far more than the average government worker and considerably more than employees with similar resumes working in comparable positions. He will doubtlessly hang on as dutiful pitchman for GM Marsella so long as the money remains above market and Marsella stays around as boss.

But what about the real thing, the power players with wealth and connections and who have the savvy to wheel-and-deal inside the local political structure? Why do players like these participate so readily in denying credit where credit is due? Take another real-life example: Buzz Koelbel, the son of a prominent builder and property owner, who serves as a vice president of the Joint Southeast Public Improvement Association (JSPIA).[3]

Sitting with the author and several business types interested in the Southeast Corridor (sitting not contributing), Koelbel learned a good deal about how RTD's light-rail program was conceived and implemented. Yet he comes across as positively whimsical, not to say downright dishonest, in the fulsome stories he spreads around about how the Metro Chamber and Denver Moves led the Southeast Corridor parade.[4]

Since Time Immemorial

Greed and vanity wrapped in the quest for money, power and prestige—each of these plays a part in ongoing deceptions. But the author, as an economist who through much of his professional life accustomed himself to assuming overly simplified human motives (Bentham-type utilitarianism and profit maximization), lacks the clinical competence needed to pull all the various parts together.[5]

Historians can help take the answer a step further. Generally dealing with *what* people did rather than *why* they did it, historians can talk about the past in ways that enlighten the present. Almost since time immemorial power-elites have stolen the personal histories of peoples they deem their inferiors. Ancient Romans stole the histories of the Celts; Great Britain stole the history of India; and Americans, lest we forget, robbed both African slaves and Native Americans of their history and culture, and even their names. A satisfactory answer to the question "why" will require the thoughts of moral philosophers, anthropologists and maybe even someone from the much maligned profession of psychoanalysis.[6] While waiting for a collaborative investigation to commence, here's a community grievance that's worth shouting from the highest mountain:

The Denver Metro Chamber and its allies never promised to tell the straight truth about light rail. They very seldom have.

Hardheads and Diehards

While the big-wheels turned mostly in rail's favor, including Republican Governor Bill Owens (see Chapter 11), clusters of smaller ones remained stuck in stubborn opposition. Among the loudest and most persistent of these, one finds radio talk-show hosts Mike Rosen (Station KOA) and Peter Boyles (Station KNUS).

Fashioning himself a centrist Republican and free-market intellectual, Rosen tells listeners that Denver light rail should have never been built because nobody rides it. Why he continues to spread such out-and-out silliness is anybody's guess. A short walk from his studio to the northwest corner of 16th and Stout Streets might encourage him to recant. This is where all day long large rail-borne crowds can be seen sweeping into and out of central downtown.

Boyles, a lesser product of the talk-show phenomenon, casts himself as a streetwise populist. He proved himself as an anti-rail fanatic early on and has never let up, panning both the idea and everyone connected with it in every conceivable way. For a time Boyles left the solidity of *terra firma* entirely behind and soared into the wild blue yonder of hallucination, claiming among other absurdities that the MAC evolved from the design board programmed to run from end to end without stopping in between for passengers. He hasn't changed his opinions, at least not in public, which leads to the question: "Who would seriously want him to?"

Nobody, really. At one time Boyles and Rosen had it within their power to jeopardize light rail. No longer. Taking off-target shots at rail today is pretty much a waste of ammunition. Denverites know a good thing when they see it. They have become too accustomed to speed and comfort, and to the singular freedom from diesel fumes, to be taken in by talk-show chatter.

Fox Versus Hedgehogs

How did RTD board members manage to climb around and through all the impediments—some of which were downright dumb but many others cleverly thought out? Resilience and a sense of humor and a thick skin—these helped a lot. As did the good sense to adopt an indispensable principle of modern life: When old theories no longer work—either predictably or heuristically—exchange them for theories that do.

Another quality strikes the author as equally crucial—a vital attribute evoked by this fragment of Greek poetry: "The fox knows many things, but the hedgehog knows one big thing." (Archilochus, circa 650 BC.)

Using this snippet as his central theme, historian/philosopher Isaiah Berlin wrote his brilliantly conceived and complexly argued study of Leo Tolstoy, *The Hedgehog and the Fox* (1953). Although Tolstoy thought of himself as a hedgehog and searched for a unifying principle into which everything he knew could be folded, he acted in practice as a natural-born fox. Therein lay his genius: His ability to depict each major character with unsurpassed particularity.

The metaphor can extend to political leaders. Joseph Stalin was a hedgehog who knew one big thing: The state should monopolize all resources—material, intellectual, spiritual. By contrast Franklin Roosevelt, a fox if there ever was one, reckoned with many smaller things: The private control of most resources shored up by state help in a broad variety of ways, notably bank-deposit insurance, social security and aggregate fiscal policies.

At the risk of tainting the sacred with the profane, the metaphor also stretches to cover light-rail development. Metro Chamber leaders and their associates comported themselves like single-minded hedgehogs throughout light-rail's creative struggles. They yearned for a full-fledged light-rail system but plodded along like one-note ideologues when it came to aligning their strategies with their desires. "The bland leading the bland," as John Kenneth Galbraith once wrote, they clung to a single ineffective theory about how to build rail, showing scant ability or even inclination to come up with something pragmatically achievable.[7]

What did work at the time was the flexible ability to solve new puzzles and juggle old components. To wit: financing within given tax rates, step-by-step corridor and alignment selection, fully tested technology, incremental buildouts. Denver's undeniably far-reaching progress over the past decade or so didn't just happen. It was brought into concrete reality by a den of sharp-eyed, strong-willed, tough-minded foxes.

The author would like to close this chapter with a keenly felt tribute to the men and women who so boldly brought Denver light rail to fruition. So with what is probably the last charge from a well-worn bugle and a hearty tally-ho he salutes each of the two-footed foxes named below:

Dan Gray (District H)   Kevin Sampson (District J)
Gloria Holliday (District B)   Helen Steele (District M)
Glenda Swanson Lyle (District B)   Cameron Winder (District E)
Bill Womack (District I)   Bernard Zimmer (District G)

All these former RTD directors, each and every one of them, can take pride in the work they did—in both their individual contributions and in their collective achievements. The author is proud to have been a foundational member of the group. Good luck to all.

Notes

1. Under the chairmanship of Rick Garcia (C), RTD's General Manager Evaluation Committee seems more like a convocation of worker bees slathering up the queen than a legislative committee representing a human society. Garcia uses the committee to demonstrate why Marsella always deserves a big raise rather than to inquire into the question of whether or not a raise of any amount is justified. Among the devices Director Garcia has used: Misleading comparative data, hand-picked consultants (as if highly paid consultants were necessary), the exclusion in evaluation reports of known anti-Marsella viewpoints.
2. Gene Amole, "Five Miles of Light Rail Will Go a Long Way," *Rocky Mountain News*, 4 April 1991.
3. JSPIA, founded in 1980, is an association of 17 special Metropolitan Districts whose overall goal is to improve mobility in Denver's southeastern business corridor.
4. There is no disposition here to single out Buzz Koelbel; he is but one among many. If the author wanted to skewer anybody on a personal level in this connection it would doubtlessly be Mile-Hi-Builders' George Thorn and the Technological Center's Ray Bullock. This duo has lived on the business/government boundary where light edges into darkness for so long they would never ask about the morality of a double cross, only about the economic return from it.
5. These simplifications don't detract from the predictive value of economic models but they do cause great misunderstanding when applied to normative issues.
6. Greek philosopher Euripides checked in early on the topic: "It is the norm for Greeks to rule barbarians." Now, that's the kind of concept the Denver Metro Chamber can buy into.
7. John Kenneth Galbraith, *The Affluent Society*, Boston; Houghton Mifflin, 1958.

14

RESTORING FREE SPEECH
The Long and Unhappy Life of RTD Censorship

W hen newly elected board chairman Bob Tonsing (H) announced during the early months of 1999 that he was creating RTD's first-ever Office of Censorship with himself wedged into the Grand Inquisitor's seat, he inadvertently let citizens in on a smarmy little secret. In exchange for the detritus of political advantage, Tonsing and allies stood ready to trample one of America's most cherished values: political free speech.

What made Tonsing and cohorts think they could successfully thumb their noses at the First Amendments to the US and Colorado Constitutions? What made them want to try? Arrogance set the stage. Money and political power played *deus ex machina*.

Free Speech Not Wanted

For starters Tonsing's crowd argued the First Amendment doesn't apply to RTD. The board majority controls all public monies flowing into the agency, they insisted, and we aren't buying any free speech. We don't need no stinkin' free speech. What's wanted around here is less independence and more togetherness, especially on the board of directors.

And that's not all, they insinuated. We're ready to use *our* money together with the hardball clout of *our* regional government to blow away anybody who goes poking around for constitutional protection. We've got the moxie and the muscle plus a rough-and-ready legal team that's always up for a rumble. Who's got the stamina and wherewithal to roll us? Certainly not the likes of Directors Gloria Holliday (B) and Jack McCroskey (A) who are the only loose-lipped directors we're currently out to silence.

Obviously Tonsing and team couldn't have strayed such a long way away from traditional American mores absent majority backing. Only Holliday and the author registered opposition. Other board members either held their tongues or signaled support.[1] Director Mary Blue (1) who followed Tonsing as chair and continued his censorship, led the cheering section. (Actually a jeering section that specialized in besmirching oppositional reputations.)

How did Chairs Tonsing and Blue defend their gag orders? Whatever happened to the tried-and-true idea of hearing all sides? When did disputing conventional wisdom turn into treasonable heresy? In this chapter we address both the political and legal aspects of these questions, paying particular attention to recent rulings by the Colorado Court of Appeals and the Colorado Supreme Court. We also note Senate Joint Resolution 02-0441, passed by the Colorado General Assembly during its regular 2002 session. We conclude with several comments on the future of public transport and light rail.

How Tonsing and Blue Pulled It Off

After taking office on 1 January 1983, the first elected board began acting pretty much like a normal American government. It moved to eliminate star-chamber proceedings, to ensure every board member an equal vote, and to encourage give-and-take debate. Without a time-tested set of procedures to guide it, the new board did occasionally find itself rowing through choppy waters. But always visible, even through the smirr of waves and rain, were the overall goals of efficiency, transparency, accountability. And in plain sight above these basics hung RTD's formal oath of office—a simple but noble statement requiring each board member to protect the US and Colorado Constitutions, including naturally the Bill of Rights.

RTD began drifting away from these righteous fundamentals during late summer 1997 with the arrival of GM Marsella. It severed all remaining ties in early 1999 when Chairman Tonsing issued the following manifesto, which embodies his intention to stamp out dissent within the board office:

> RTD board resources, including staff assistants and mate-rials, are available in support of directors' activities that clearly have to do with carrying out the agency's respon-sibilities under state law, and RTD by-laws and directives. Accordingly, I have directed the board staff not to pro-vide such support when any reasonable person would conclude that other agendas (some of which might in fact hinder the RTD mission) are at work.[2]

Consciously misnamed a "resource policy," Tonsing's edict found immediate favor among the entire board (excepting Holliday and the author) and was enthusiastically embraced by GM Marsella and his key aides. The bureaucracy liked the order because it immunized them from criticism. Reasons for the board's acceptance are not as easy to get a handle on, but part of the reason has to do with paranoia. Sayings such as "Don't spill the beans" and "Don't unsettle the soup" assumed the mantle of institutional wisdom. Squishy clichés such as "Let's not wash our dirty laundry in public" hardened into mandatory guidelines.

Crucial Distinction

Tonsing's directive needs precious little interpretation and virtually no reading between the lines. He says what he means straight out. He's setting himself up to control what board members can say and to decide which board-member opinions will see print.

His actions might pass legal muster were he the proprietor of a privately owned business firm. But he isn't. RTD represents a citizen-owned government, and Tonsing accounts for but one of

15 popularly elected directors. The distinction between private and public is crucial:

> *The First Amendment clearly protects the speech of public officials discussing public policies within the forum to which they were duly elected.*[3]

So what's Tonsing's problem? Does he not grasp the meaning of "political free speech" as defined by the First Amendment? Or does he think that while the Constitution works just fine for "little people" (á la Leona Helmsley) it doesn't govern either him or his comrade-in-arms Chairwoman Blue? Whatever the source of Tonsing's cynical confusion, the Colorado Court of Appeals has discussed the question in a way that leaves the issue's every facet glittering in crystal clarity.

Here is a digest of the appellate court's exceptionally searching and lucid (and unanimous) ruling:

• On 27 September 2001, the Colorado Court of Appeals rendered a decision in the case of *Holliday/McCroskey v. Regional Transportation District*, Court of Appeals No. 00CA 1778 (Colo. App. 2001), ordering the trial court to proceed with consideration of claims by two RTD directors. These directors claimed their speech rights were denied and their federal civil rights were violated by RTD's policy denying them access to the RTD resources they needed to disseminate correspondence unfavorable to RTD.

• On 15 April 2002, the Colorado Supreme Court denied RTD's petition for *certiorari*. This ruling made the Court of Appeals decision the final judicial pronouncement at the time.

• The decision reviewed the content and implementation of RTD's policy denying the plaintiffs access to staff assistance and materials, " . . . *specifically the withholding of typing services for correspondence to state officials and news media containing criticism of RTD light-rail policies, allegations of conflict of interest, waste and mismanagement, calling for termination of officers and discussion of RTD bond-ballot issues.*"[4]

• Noting that government may regulate speech in non-public forums in order to preserve these forums for their intended purposes, the court nonetheless stated that such regulations must draw distinctions that are both reasonable and viewpoint neutral. *It also held that the case presents genuine issues of material fact "as to whether the distinctions drawn by defendants are viewpoint neutral."*

• The plaintiffs alleged that their letters were not typed because the defendants disagreed with the contents of these letters. The court also stated that the evidence raises issues " . . . *concerning whether the resources policy as applied is an instance of pure viewpoint discrimination that the First Amendment cannot abide."*

• The court went on to illustrate that viewpoint discrimination contravening the exercise of First Amendment rights is particularly unfortunate when it restrains the criticism of government actions, noting " . . . *that there is practically universal agreement that a major purpose of the First Amendment is to protect the free discussion of governmental affairs. For speech concerning public affairs is more than self-expression; it is the essence of self government."*

• The court cited at length from the United States Supreme Court decision in *Bond v. Floyd*, 385 US 116 (1966), to the effect that elected officials should receive the "widest latitude to express their views on the issues of public policy." The court further stated, " . . . *legislators have an obligation to take positions on controversial political questions so that their constituents can be fully informed by them, and be better able to address their qualifications for office; also so that they may be represented in governmental debates by the person they have elected to represent them.*"

• The court rejected the defendants' claims that their policy involved minimal restriction on free speech, writing that " . . . *once the RTD provided funding and resources to Directors to communicate with their constituents and others, it could not selectively foreclose this or other viewpoints regarding RTD business.*"

• The court also noted that causes of action existed under a federal civil rights statute against RTD and the executive assistant to the RTD board in both the assistant's official and individual capacities, " . . . *subjecting the executive assistant to personal liability for acts that the assistant would be expected to know violate constitutional protections.*" (See Appendix F for the Colorado Court of Appeals' full decision.)

General Assembly Weighs In

Reviewing the Appellate Court's ruling and the Supreme Court's decision to uphold that ruling, the Colorado General Assembly considered RTD's constitution-defying censorship during its 2002 session. This review resulted in Senate Joint Resolution 02-044 entitled: *Concerning the Support of the General Assembly for Constitutional Protections Accorded Elected Officials in Expressing Their Voices on Public Issues.*

Introduced by Senate Minority Leader Senator John Andrews (R) and Chairman of the House Judiciary Committee Representative Shawn Mitchel (R), the measure reads in part:

> That the General Assembly expresses full support and endorsement of the principles of free speech announced by the Colorado Court of Appeals in the case of *Holliday/McCroskey v. Regional Transportation District*, especially as those principles relate to prohibiting viewpoint discrimination, allowing elected officials the widest latitude to express their views on issues of public policy, and promoting the free discussion of important policy differences that directly affect the public. The General Assembly further recommends other legislative bodies of the state accord the free speech rights of their own elected officials the highest degree of protection consistent with the law.

The Senate voted favorably 35 to 0; the House 59 to 5. This decision represents a Colorado landmark. For the first time in its 125-year history the Colorado General Assembly passed a resolution directly rebuking an elected local government. (The full text may be found in Appendix F.)

Humphrey, Fulbright, McCain

In verbal arguments before the Court of Appeals, RTD attorney Marla Lien asserted that the US Congress can and should emulate RTD's wretched example—that is, congressional majorities need not let minorities use Congress' clerical and mailing facilities. Further, as if to secure her role as chief spokesperson for RTD officialdom, she hurriedly added that US courts need not reproduce and distribute minority opinions.[5]

All of which, although not quite as gormless as her written briefs claiming that censorship is merely a type of scarce-resource allocation, shows which way RTD's moral wind is blowing: toward intolerance and depotism.

Now, while there isn't the slightest disposition here to suggest that Lien's mordant notions will ever prevail (pray on it), one might ruminate on how several highly significant issues might have played out had her un-American proposals gone into effect 50 years ago.

- **Senator Hubert Humphrey**, Democrat from Minnesota, couldn't have brought to fruition his transforming but hotly contested ideas about Civil Rights.

- **Senator J. William Fulbright**, Democrat from Arkansas, couldn't have presented his formidable but sharply controversial views on the Vietnam War.

- **Senator John McCain**, Republican from Arizona, couldn't have fought the good fight and scored an amazing victory for election reform.

Just one parting thought about attorney Marla Lien and RTD's legal department: Private attorneys devise all manner of fanciful claims for their clients without damage to their own reputations. But should government lawyers like Lien receive supersized, tax-funded salaries to debase Civil Rights?[6] The question needs asking partly because of Lien's disquieting performance.

Less fastidious than your average lawyer about personal probity, Lien first conferred with Tonsing about how to stifle free speech. She then defended the intrigue in court by bizarrely arguing that putting a lid on expression is just another way of managing the budget. Finally, after this palpable nonsense flunked the Appellate Court's intelligence tests, Lien told the Colorado Supreme Court that so-called "government speech" trumps individual speech. Once government has spoken, according to Lien, non-conforming elected officials become legally obliged to stick a sock in their mouths and practice running on all fours. Wrong, egregiously wrong. No matter how much RTD's higher-ups may desire it, free speech is not moribund in Colorado.

Censoring Abolitionists

While freedom-denying theories such as those expounded by RTD are considered secularly blasphemous over most of America today, there was once a place and a time when these ideas would have fit right in.[7] Glance backward to the American South during the half-century before the Civil War (1861-1865). For many Southerners, slavery constituted the accepted way of life. Field slaves made the economic wheels go around; house slaves offered a diurnal touch of comfort and luxury; slave ownership provided the prevailing measure of self-esteem and social standing. Not surprisingly most slavers bent every effort to shield their "peculiar institution" from criticism.

But above the Mason-Dixon Line there were abolitionists who not only abhorred the peculiar institution, but who insisted on talking about it. They inundated the North with antislavery meetings and speeches; they flooded the South with mailings of antislavery letters and literature. The slave power couldn't spoil many meetings or squelch many speeches, but it could stop the mailings. This it accomplished through rigorous censorship. Southern officials told their postmasters to open and inspect mail from the North and to embargo everything expressing antislavery sentiments. By doing as told, the US Postal Service helped keep the national disgrace of human bondage under wraps for some 50 shadowy years—thereby possibly delaying and almost certainly intensifying the gathering storm.

Why did slave owners resort to censorship? This question these slavers answered quite candidly. They were mortally afraid their human chattel might spy a bit of abolitionist literature, decipher a few pages, better comprehend their condition, and then rise in holy rebellion.

Today, in a similar spirit, one might inquire into what it is that RTD censors fear so much. (Censors are always afraid of something, having no authentic idea of what it takes to live unafraid.) Exactly which ". . . goblins will get 'ya if 'ya don't watch out!!"[8] The goblins of honesty, understanding, public service? One gets the feeling that many people engaged in the spineless game of "scaredy-cat cover-up" (specifically Tonsing and Blue and their sympathizers) would very much enjoy burning such witches.

From a legalistic viewpoint the South's free-speech denial stood on firmer grounds than did RTD's later actions. Antebellum scholars could maintain that First Amendment restrictions against government infringement of speech applied to federal actions only. With ratification of the Fourteenth Amendment in 1868, state governments and their local units were specifically compelled to respect free speech, too.

The conclusions to be drawn? RTD had no business whatsoever in abridging director speech. Officials knew the rules full well, but proceded to do whatever they wanted to do, "To hell with the Constitution!" they all but shouted. The culpability of these actions is inescapable.

A few slavers, echoed by some RTD officials, pitched an attenuated sort of censorship. Whereas it may be acceptable to criticize reigning authority, the thinking goes, this must be done kindly, gingerly and with a mouth full of flannel. To which famed abolitionist William Lloyd Garrison responded with raw honesty and in a praiseworthy breach of etiquette: *I have a need to be all on fire, for I have mountains of ice about me to melt.*"[9]

Confession versus Worms

Introduced into RTD by Chairman Tonsing's pronouncement of 15 February 1999, political censorship departed these environs, formally at least, on 20 August 2002. The occasion was passage of RTD Resolution 33 wherein the board agreed to stop flouting the Constitution.[10] Henceforward, board members said, we will happily allow free speech within our offices. "Well not happily, perhaps, but under court duress we will countenance it."

During the more than three years between the above dates, the democratic virtues of free speech and openness were more than just ignored: They were conspicuously dishonored day after day, week after week. How can this be? The denial of political free speech represents the repudiation of representative government. Democracies thrive on open debate; they perish without it. So how can elected officials pledged to honor the Constitution deliberately undercut it? Take away free expression and the American legacy crashes—all of it, including fair elections, sound judgment, individual liberty. Without free speech everything in the American political system from top to bottom falls into pieces, and the pieces metamorphose into tyranny.

Yet a pack of RTD officials sought to pare speech down to a nubbin. Toward what end? To grab onto what earlier elected boards would have scorned as a mess of pottage—a bit of economic gain, a whiff of personal power. Nor has current RTD leadership faced up to its lawlessness. Today's leaders won't let themselves acknowledge their mistakes—or come to terms with their ill-will and bad faith. Readers will recognize the type. Such people simply will not admit to wrongdoing. They will not apologize to the individuals they have harmed.[11] They would rather eat worms.

Well, our morality play has another act before denouement—the upcoming free-speech trial in Denver District Courtroom 19, scheduled for 28 July 2003. Maybe defendants—Chairs Bob Tonsing and Mary Blue and Administrative-Assistant Brenda Bergman—will decide sometime before the play's final curtain that the healing balm of confession and atonement beats the grungy taste of worm. One must hope for such signs of improvement, however small and faintly imprinted. More than three decades ago Denverites decided that public transport was too important to do without (see Chapter 7). We can rest assured they consider it positively essential today.

Saving RTD, Expanding Light Rail

Although its current leadership should be expelled at the earliest possible moment, RTD itself remains well worth saving. There's a crying need for a fresh take on both procedures and promises, but it would be a serious mistake to contemplate dismantling the entire institution. Despite its inadequacies and lapses, RTD remains the region's best hope for better public transport.

Better transport is in turn the most propitious way to make the Denver area easier to get around in, and hence a pleasanter and more attractive place in which to live. Light rail—with its locally demonstrated record of dependable, efficacious and environmentally friendly service—is central to unlocking the possibilities.

In order to press the light-rail case, one might speculate about the likelihood of future horrors, including quantum leaps in gasoline prices. But dire forecasts such as these seem superfluous.[12] Present and worsening congestion trends should by themselves prove enough to persuade the vast majority of farsighted citizens— and enough even to inspire more than a few rail-hating and smother-loving fanatics to reexamine their priorities.

Paying for the Future

How shall Metro Denver citizens pay for light-rail expansion? Sales-tax increases may come into play someday, but they weren't needed during the recent past and odds are they won't be required in the immediate future. This means that tax hikes can wait until at least 2008, and probably later.

The Denver Metro Chamber of Commerce and its close allies, including most current RTD board members, will doubtlessly disagree with the forgoing conclusion. But then what else is new?

With just one trick in its public-transport repertoire (higher tax levies), the Chamber's thinking has changed remarkably little over the past three decades. Meanwhile, the RTD board of directors has let itself fall ever more completely under the Chamber's sway. The Chamber should say and do whatever it wants, naturally, but publicly elected RTD board members ought to snap out of their dogmatic slumber and look at the situation, clear-eyed and independently. Tax-hike elections have gotten light rail exactly nowhere while step-by-step incrementalism has demonstrated a thoroughly substantiated ability to drive light rail onward-and-upward.

The figures in the space below, originally broached in Chapter 8, attest both to what works and what does not. Scorekeeping comparisons between the two numbers offer convincing reasons to keep on keeping on with step-by-step buildouts.

Total Track Miles From Three Sales-Tax Elections. **0.0**

Total Track Miles From Incremental Buildouts. **35.4**

* * *

"Free speech represents the very dignity of what a human being is . . . That's what marks us off from the stones and the stars. You can speak freely . . . It is the thing that marks us as just below the angels."

Mario Savio in *The Free Speech Movement*

Notes

1. Other Directors who either spoke in favor or acquiesced were: Karen Benker (M); Bob Briggs (J); Carl Erickson (E); Alan Fleming (D); Rick Garcia (C); Dick McLean (O); Stephen Millard (N); David E. Rose (K); Loren Sloane (G); Dick Sargent (L).

2. *Holliday and McCroskey v. Regional Transportation District,* Colorado's Court of Appeals No. 00CA1778 (Colo. App. 2001.)

3. This is by no means all the speech protected by the First Amendment. It is merely the part that seems germane to the present discussion.

4. Virtually impervious to discussion of possible waste and mismanagement, Chairman Tonsing becomes ever more agitated when confronted with issues of race relations and civil rights. The mere mention of the topics turns him livid and ulcerous, and leaves him fulminating against directors who he claims seek to raise the specter of "social unrest." Both RTD and the author possess, unfortunately, large collections of the man's diatribes.

5. Oral arguments before the Colorado Court of Appeals, Denver, Colorado, 4 September 2001.

6. RTD's budget shows that the legal department (office) was given $11.1 million to cover all its activities during 2001. Department managers will deny it, naturally, but very considerable savings could be realized through privatization. The department is headed by Jack Kennedy, a life-long bureaucrat-lawyer. Since he joined RTD, moving from Washington, D.C., during the middle 1980s, Kennedy has almost always advised the board to conceal whatever can be concealed, and to reveal only what must be revealed. It has been said of Kennedy: "Such time as he can spare from nodding in his office, he devotes to the neglect of his duties."

7. Michael Kent Curtis, *Free Speech, The People's Darling Amendment,* Durham & London: Duke University Press, 2000.

8. James Whitcomb Riley, *Little Orphan Annie,* NY; Putnam Publishing, 1983.

9. Henry Mayer, *All on Fire,* NY; St. Martin's Press, 1998.

10. RTD Resolution 33, Series of 2002, Denver; August 2002. Held in RTD files.

11. Aside from the trauma of being arbitrarily cast down from an elected RTD director to a position of reduced influence and stolen liberties, what lingers uppermost in the author's memory about these events is the unending and unsavory delight Bob Tonsing, Mary Blue and Brenda Bergman took from exploiting their dictatorial domination. The unjust taking of civil liberties is never uplifting—not for the predators and not for the victims most certainly. Writing about these events even now, several years after the fact, races the pulse, churns the stomach, and opens the portals for angina.

12. For a treasure-trove of urban scare-mongering, see: Miles Davis, *Dead Cities*, NY; The New Press, 2002. Especially the section entitled "The Subway That Ate L.A."

15

ENDNOTE

Omnibus Jaunts and Drivers

One phase of those days [1846 and '47] must by no means go unrecorded—namely the Broadway omnibuses...and the men specifically identified with them and giving vitality and meaning to them—the drivers . . . a strange, natural, quick-eyed and wondrous race (not only Rabelais and Cervantes would have gloated upon them but Homer and Shakespeare would).

How well I remember them. How many hours, forenoon and afternoons—now perhaps June or July, in cooler air riding the whole length of Broadway, the most vivid yarns ever spun and the rarest mimicry—or perhaps I declaimed some stormy passage from Julius Caesar or Richard (you could roar as loudly as you choose in that heavy, dense, uninterrupted street.)

Yes, I knew all the drivers then, Broadway Jack, Dressmaker, George Storms, Old Elephant, his brother Young Elephant (who came afterward), Tippy, Pop Rice, Big Frank, Yellow Joe, Pete Callahan, Patsy Dee and dozens more; for there were hundreds. They had immense qualities eating, drinking, women, great personal pride in their way perhaps a few slouches here and there but I should have trusted the general run of them in their simple good will and honor under all circumstances. Not only for comradeship and sometimes affection, great studies I found them also.

I suppose the critics will laugh heartily but the influence of those Broadway omnibus jaunts and drivers and declamations and escapades undoubtedly extend into the gestation of Leaves of Grass.

Walt Whitman
Speciman Days, 1892

Appendix A

LOCAL IMPROVEMENT AND SERVICE DISTRICTS

REGIONAL TRANSPORTATION DISTRICT ACT

(Senate Bill No. 309. By Senators Bermingham, H.Fowler, Vollack, Strickland, Decker, Kemp, Nicholson, and Williams; also Representative Byrant.)

AN ACT

CONCERNING PUBLIC TRANSIT

Be it enacted by the General Assembly of the State of Colorado: Section 1. Chapter 89, Colorado Revised Statues 1963, as amended is amended BY THE ADDITION OF A NEW ARTICLE to read:

ARTICLE 20

REGIONAL TRANSPORTATION DISTRICT ACT

89-20-1. Short title.--This article shall be known and may be cited as the "Regional Transportation District Act".

89-20-2. Declaration of purpose.--(1) (a) The general assembly hereby determines, finds, and declares:

(b) That the creation of the regional transportation district will promote the public health safety convenience, economy, and welfare of the residents of the district and of the state of Colorado and

(c) That a general law cannot be made applicable to the district and to the properties, powers, duties, functions, privileges, immunities, rights, liabilities, and disabilities of such district as provided in this article because of a number of atypical factors and special conditions concerning same

89-20-3. Definitions.--(1) As used in this article unless the context clearly indicates otherwise:

(2) "District" means the regional transportation district created by this article.

(3) "Board" means the board of directors of the district.

(4) "Director" means a member of the board.

(5) "Person" means any natural person, association, partnership, company, or corporation.

(6) "Public body" means the state of Colorado or any county, city and county, city town district or any other political subdivision of the state, excluding the regional transportation district.

(7) "Taxpaying elector" means a person qualified to vote in general elections in the state, who is resident of the district and who is an owner of real or personal property within the boundaries of the district which property is subject to taxation at the time of any election held under the provisions of this article or at any other time in reference to which the term "taxpaying elector" is used. A person who is obligated to pay taxes under contract to purchase real property in the district shall be considered as an owner. The ownership of any property subject to the payment of a specific ownership tax on a motor vehicle or trailer or of any other excise or

property tax other than general ad valorem property taxes shall not constitute the ownership of property subject to taxation as provided in this article.

(8) "Taxes" or "taxation" means general ad valorem property taxes only.

(9) "Revenues" means the tolls, fees, rates, charges, or other income and revenues derived from the operation of the mass transportation system of the district and income derived from investments by the district.

(10) "Operation and maintenance expenses" means all reasonable and necessary current expenses of the district, paid or accrued, of operating, maintaining, and repairing facilities of the mass transportation system of the district.

(11) "Net revenues" means the revenues after the deduction of operation and maintenance expenses.

(12) "Condemn" or "condemnation" means the exercise by the district of the power of eminent domain to acquire mass transportation facilities and property, real or personal, for the public use of the district.

(13) "Publication" means the publication once a week for three consecutive weeks in at least one newspaper having general circulation in the district. Publication need not be made on the same day of the week in each of the three weeks except that not less than fourteen days shall intervene between the first day of publication and the last day of publication.

(14) "District securities" means bonds, temporary bonds, refunding bonds, special obligation bonds, interim notes, notes, and warrants of the district authorized to be issued by this article.

(15) "Mass transportation system" means any system which transports the general public by bus, rail, air, or by any other means of conveyance, or any combination thereof, along prescribed routes, except any railroad subject to the "Federal Railway Labor Act", Title 45, U. S. C.

89.20-4. **Creation of district.**--There is hereby created a district to be known and designated as the "Regional Transportation District".

89-20-5. **District area.**--The area comprising the district shall consist of the city and county of Denver and the counties of Adams, Arapahoe, Jefferson, Boulder, Weld, and Douglas.

89-20-6. **Mass transportation system.--adoption of comprehensive plan.--**
(1) The district acting by and through the board, is hereby authorized, empowered, and directed, subject to section 89-20-7, to develop, maintain, and operate a mass transportation system for the benefit of the inhabitants of the district.
(2) When a comprehensive plan for the development, maintenance, and operation of as proposed mass transportation system for the district is available to the board and satisfactory- to the board, it shall be tentatively adopted. Such a plan may be prepared by the board or by any other person under the control of the board. The board may incorporate into such comprehensive plan any plans prepared and proposed by any person, organization, public body, or the federal government. The plan shall be prepared in such a manner as to coordinate the proposed mass transportation system with other aspects of transportation in the district, including state and county highways and arterial streets.
(3) The board shall schedule a public hearing on the tentatively adopted plan and shall give notice of such hearing by publication. After the hearing and any adjournments thereof, the

board may adopt changes in the tentatively adopted plan or approve the plan as tentatively adopted. If any substantial changes in the plan as tentatively adopted are proposed by the board, it shall schedule further hearings and shall give notice thereof by publication. If at any time the board proposes substantial changes in the adopted plan, it shall schedule a public hearing thereon and shall give notice thereof by publication.

89-20-7. Authorizing election.--Within five years from the effective date of This article, unless there is pending in any court an action ques-tioning the validity of this article or any part thereof or the power of the district to proceed under this article, there shall be submitted to the taxpaying electors of the district a question authorizing the district to incur debt and to issue securities of the district therefor, for the purpose of developing a mass transportation system for the district. If a majority- of the taxpaying electors of the district voting on the question do not approve the incurrence of debt and the issuance of the bonds by the district as provided in the question, the board shall wind up the affairs of the district and shall cause it to be dissolved as provided in section 89-20-58.

89-20-8. Board of directors.--The governing body of the district shall be a board of directors consisting of twenty-one taxpaying electors of the district as follows: Ten directors from the city and county of Denver, two directors each from the counties of Adams, Arapahoe, Jefferson, and Boulder, one director each from the counties of Weld and Douglas, and one at-large director. The board of directors shall be appointed as provided in sections 89-20-9, 89-20-10, and 89-20-11. All powers, duties, functions, rights, and privileges vested in the district shall lie exercised and performed by the board; except :hat the exercise of any executive, administrative, or ministerial powers may be delegated by the board to officers and employees of the district. Except for the first board of directors appointed pursuant to section 89-20-9 and except for any director appointed to fill a vacancy pursuant to section 89-20-11, the term of office of each director shall commence on July 1 next following his appointment or as soon thereafter as he may qualify, and shall be for four years.

89-20-9. Initial board.--(1) (a) Upon the effective date of this article, or as soon thereafter as possible, the boards of county commissioners of the counties of Adams, Arapahoe, Jefferson, and Boulder shall appoint t two taxpaying electors each to the district board, and the boards of county commissioners of the counties of Weld and Douglas shall appoint one taxpaying elector each to the district board. The mayor of the city and county of Denver, subject to the approval of city council of the city and county of Denver, shall appoint ten taxpaying electors to the district board. The at-large appointee shall be chosen by the twenty appointees hereinabove provided for. Appointments to the initial board shall be made as follows:

(b) Five appointees from the city and county of Denver, and one each from the counties of Adams, Arapahoe, Jefferson, Boulder, and the appointee from the county of Douglas shall be appointed for terms expiring on July 1, 1971.

(c) Five appointees from the city and county of Denver, and one each from the counties of Adams, Arapahoe, Jefferson, Boulder, and the appointee from the county of Weld shall be appointed for terms expiring on July 1, 1973.

(d) Initial and subsequent appointments to the district board by the individual boards of county commissioners shall require approval of a majority of the governing bodies of the cities and towns located within or partially within the county.

(2) Upon their appointment, the directors shall meet, qualify, and elect by an affirmative vote of eleven, a taxpaying elector of the district who shall be known as the at-large director. The term of office of the at-large director shall expire on July 1, 1973

89-20-10.--Subsequent appointments to board.--Subsequent appointments to the board shall be made by the appointing authorities set forth in section 89-20-9 in June of the year in which the term of office of the director expires. Subsequent elections and appointments of the at-large director shall be held and made in July of the year in which such director's term has expired.

89-20-11--Vacancies. A change of residence of a member of the board to a place outside the district shall automatically create a vacancy on the board. Upon a vacancy occurring in the board by reason of death, change of residence, resignation, or for any other reason other than expiration of term, the appointing authorities set forth in section 89-20-9 shall appoint a taxpaying elector of the district to fill the vacancy for the unexpired term.

89-20-12.--Fidelity bonds. Each director shall, before entering upon his official duties, give a fidelity bond to the district in the sum of ten thousand dollars with good and sufficient surety, to be approved by the governor, conditioned for the faithful performance of the duties of his office. Premiums on all fidelity bonds provided for in this section shall be paid by the district and filed in the office of the secretary of state.

89-20-13.--Board's administrative powers. (1) (a) The board shall have the following administrative powers:

(b) To fix the time and place, or places, at which its regular meetings, to be held at least quarterly, shall be held within the district and shall provide for the calling and holding of special meetings.

(c) To adopt and amend bylaws and rules for procedure.

(d) To elect one director as chairman of the board and another director as chairman pro tom of the board, and to appoint one or more persons as secretary and treasurer of the board.

(e) To prescribe a system of business administration, to create neces-sary offices, and to establish the powers, duties, and compensation of all officers, agents, and employees and other persons contracting with the district, subject to the provi-sions of section 89-20-16.

(f) To prescribe a method of auditing and allowing or rejecting claims and demands.

(g) To provide a method for the letting of contracts on a fair and competitive basis for the construction of works, any facility, or any project, or any interest therein, or the performance or furnishing of labor, materials, or supplies as required in this article.

(h) To designate an official newspaper published in the district in the English language; except that nothing contained in this article shall prevent the board from directing publication in any additional newspaper where it deems that the public necessity may so require.

(i) To make and pass resolutions and orders necessary in order to carry out the provisions of this article.

89-20-14. Records of board.--All resolutions and orders shall be recorded and authenticated by the signature of the presiding officer of the board and the secretary. Every legislative act of the board of a general or permanent nature shall be by resolution. The book of resolutions and orders shall be a public record. A record shall also be made of all other proceedings of the board, minutes of the meetings, certificates, contracts, bonds given by officers, employees, and any other agents of the district, and all corporate acts, which record shall also be a public record. The treasurer shall keep an account of all moneys received by and disbursed on behalf of the district, which shall also be a public record. Any public record of the district: shall be open for inspection by any taxpaying elector of the district, or by any representative of the state, or any county, city and county, city, or town within the district. All records are subject to audit as provided by law for political subdivisions.

89-20-15. Meetings of board.--All meetings of the board shall be held within the district and shall be open to the public. No business of the board shall be transacted except at a regular or special meeting at which a quorum consisting of at least a majority of the total membership of the board is present. Any action of the board shall require the affirmative vote of eleven members present and voting.

89-20-16. Compensation of directors.--Each director shall receive as compensation for his services a sum not in excess of six hundred dollars per annum, as fixed be the board. No director shall receive any compensation as an officer, engineer, attorney, employee, or other agent of the district. Nothing contained in this article shall be construed as preventing the board from authorizing the reimbursement of any director for expenses incurred and appertaining to the activities of the district.

89-20-17. Conflicts in interest prohibited.--No director, officer, employee, or agent of the district shall be interested in any contract or transaction with the district except in his official representative capacity.

89-20-18. Additional powers of district.--(1) (a) In addition to any other powers granted to the district in this article, the district shall have the following powers:

(b) To have the duties, privileges, immunities, rights, liabilities, and disabilities of a public body politic and corporate. The district shall be a political subdivision of the state.

(c) To have perpetual existence and succession, subject to the provi-sions of sections 89-20-7 and 89-20-61.

(d) To adopt, have, and use a seal and to alter same at pleasure.

(e) To sue and be sued.

(f) To enter into any contract or agreement not inconsistent with this article or the laws of this state.

(g) To borrow money and to issue district securities evidencing same.

(h) To refund any loan or obligation of the district and to issue refunding securities therefor.

(i) To purchase, trade, exchange, or otherwise acquire, maintain, and dispose of real property and personal property and any interest therein.

(j) To levy and cause to be collected taxes on all taxable proper-ty within the district, subject to the limitations imposed by this article and the laws of the state.

(k) To employ such officers, agents, employees, and other persons necessary to carry out the purposes of this article and to acquire office space, equipment, services, supplies, and insurance necessary to carry out the purposes of this article.

(l) To condemn property for public use.

(m) To establish, maintain, and operate a mass transportation system and all necessary facilities relating thereto within the district across or along any public street, highway, bridge, viaduct, or other public right-of-way, or in, upon, under, or over any vacant public lands without first obtaining a franchise from the public body having jurisdiction over same; except that the district shall cooperate with any public body having such jurisdiction and the district shall promptly restore any such street, highway, bridge, viaduct, or other public right-of-way to its former state f usefulness as nearly as may be and shall not use the same in such manner as to impair completely or unnecessarily the usefulness thereof.

(n) To fix and from time to time increase or decrease the revenues for services and facilities provided by the district; to pledge net revenues for the payment of special district obligation bonds which have been issued in accordance with :his article; and to enforce the collection of such revenues. Revenues for services and facilities provided by the district shall be so set as to pay all operation and maintenance expenses of the district.

(o) To deposit any moneys of the district in any banking institution within or without the district.

(p) To invest any surplus money in the district's treasury, including moneys in a sinking or reserve fund established for the purpose of retiring any district securities, not required for immediate necessities of the district in its own district securities or federal or state securities.

(q) To sell from time to time such securities thus purchased and held.

(r) To accept grants or loans from the federal government, to enter into contracts and cooperate with the federal government, and to do any and all things necessary, not inconsistent with this article or the laws of this state, .n order to avail itself of such aid, assistance, and cooperation under any federal legislation now or hereafter enacted.

(s) To enter into joint operating or service contracts, and acquisition, improvement, equipment, or disposal contracts with any public body in the district concerning any mass transportation facility whether acquired by the district or by the public body; to perform such contracts; and to accept grants and contributions from any public body—or any other person in connection therewith.

(t) To enter upon any land within the district to make surveys, borings, soundings, and examinations for the purposes of the district.

(u) To have the management control, and supervision of all business and affairs relating to any mass transportation facility authorized in this article, or otherwise concerning the district, and of the acquisition, improvement, equipment operation, maintenance, and disposal of any property relating to any such mass transportation facility.

(v) To enter into contracts of indemnity and guaranty.

(w) To secure financial statements, appraisals, economic feasibility reports, and valuations of any type relating to the mass transportation system of the district or any facility therein.

(x) To make all contracts, execute all instruments, and do all things necessary or convenient in the exercise of the powers granted in this article, or in the performance of the district's covenants or duties, or in order to secure the payment of district securities.

(y) To have and exercise all rights and powers necessary or incidental to or implied from the specific powers granted in this article, which specific powers shall not be considered as at limitation upon any power necessary or appropriate to carry out the purposes and intent of this article.

(z) To exercise all or any part or combination of the powers granted in this article.

89-20-19, Levy of taxes--limitations.--(1) Notwithstanding any other provision of law or this article to the contrary no taxes shall be levied directly or indirectly, be the district under provisions of this article unless such levy is solely for the payment of a debt of the district, the incurrence of which debt has been authorized in advance by the tax-paying electors of the distract at an election for that purpose, as provided in this article, or for the payment of any annual deficit, if any, in the operation and maintenance expenses of the district, such levy not to exceed two on each dollar of valuation for each year, or for the payment of the actual costs incurred under sections 89-20-6, 89-20-7, and 89-20-58, such levy not to exceeded one-half mill on each dollar of valuation for assessment each year.

(2) Annually, the board shall determine the amount of money necessary to be raised by taxation for the coming year and

shall fix a rate of levy, subject to the provisions of subsection (1) of this section which rate when levied upon every dollar of valuation for assessment of taxable property within the district, together with any other unencumbered revenues and moneys of the district, shall raise that sum necessary to pay in full all interest and principal on securities of the district, except special obligations payable solely from the net revenues of the district, coming due within the coming year.

(3) The board shall certify to the counties of the district and the city and county of Denver, prior to such date or dates as may he provided by law for such counties and city and county of Denver for the levying of taxes the rate so fixed in subsection (2) of this section with directions to such counties and city and county of Denver, to levy and collect such other taxes upon the taxable property within their respective counties or city and county and to levy and collect such other taxes pursuant to section 89-20-20.

89-20-20. Levies to cover deficiencies.--In the event that the sum pro-duced from the levies authorized by section 89-20-19, together with any unencumbered revenues and moneys of the district, are insufficient to pay when due installments on contracts and securities of the district, and interest thereon, and to pay defaults and deficiencies, the board shall make such additional levies of taxes as may be necessary, subject to the provisions of section 89-20-19 (1), until such contracts and securities, and interest thereon, shall be fully paid. No levies shall be made pursuant to this section to pay any amount of special obligations of the district payable solely from the net revenues of the district.

89-20-21. Levying and collecting taxes--lien.--It shall be the duty of the body having authority to levy taxes within each county or city and county of the district to levy the taxes provided in sections 89-20-19 and 89-20-20. It shall be the duty of all officials charged with the duty of collecting taxes to collect such taxes at the time and in the form and manner and with like interest and penalties as other taxes are collected, and when collected, to pay the same to the district. The payment of such collec-tion shall be made as soon as practical after collection to the treasurer of the district zone, paid into the depository thereof to the credit of the district. All taxes levied under this article, together with interest thereon and penalties for default in payment thereof, and all costs of collecting the same, shall constitute, until paid, a perpetual lien on and against the property taxed, and such lien shall be on a parity with the tax lien of other taxes.

89-20-22. Delinquent taxes.--If the taxes levied are not paid, then delin-quent real property shall be sold at the regular tax sale for the payment of said taxes, interest and penalties, in the manner provided by the statutes of the state for selling real property for the nonpayment of taxes. If there are no bids at said tax sale for the property so offered, said property shall be struck off to the county, and the county shall account to the district in the same manner as provided by law for accounting for school, town and city taxes. Delinquent per-sonal property shall be distrained and sold as provided by law, Nothing contained in this article shall be construe, as pre-venting the collection in full of the proceeds of any and all levies of taxes lawfully made by the district, including with-out limitation, any delinquencies, interest, penalties, and costs.

89-20-23. Forms of borrowing.--Subject to the provisions of this article, the district, to carry out the purposes of this arti-cle, may borrow money and may issue the following district securities to evidence such borrowing: Notes, warrants, bonds, temporary bonds, refunding bonds, special obligation bonds, and interim notes.

89-20-24. Issuance of notes.--Subject to sections 89-20-19 (1) and 89-20-37, the district may borrow money in anticipation of taxes or revenues, or both, and issue notes to evidence the amount so borrowed.

89-20-25. Issuance of warrants.--Subject to sections 89-20-19 (1) and 89-20-37, the district may defray the cost of any services, or supplies, equipment, or other materials furnished to or for the benefit of the district by the issuance of warrant, to evidence the amount due therefor in antic-ipation of taxes or revenues, or both.

89-20-26. Maturities of notes and warrants.--Notes and warrants may mature at such time or times not exceeding one year from the respective dates of their issuance as the board may determine. They shall not be extended or funded except by the issuance of bonds, special obligation bonds, or interim notes in compliance with sections 89-20-27, 89-20-28, and 89-20-30.

89-20-27. Incurrence of special obligations.--The district may borrow money in anticipation of the revenues of the district, but not the proceeds of any taxes, and to issue special obligation bonds to evidence the amount so borrowed. Any special obligation bonds or other obligations payable solely from the net revenues of the district may be issued or incurred without an election in anticipation of such net revenues, after provision is made for defying all current operation and maintenance expenses of all mass transportation facilities of the district and other operation expenses of the district. Nothing contained in this article shall be construed as preventing the district from submitting to the taxpaying electors of the district any question authorizing the issuance of such special obligation bonds or otherwise incurring such special obligations.

89-20-28. Incurrence of debt.--(1) Subject to sections 89-20-19 (1) and 89-20-87 and subsection (2) of this section, the district may borrow money at anticipation of taxes, or both taxes and revenues and to issue bonds to evidence the amount so borrowed.

(2) No bonded indebtedness nor any other obligations which are possibly payable from the proceeds of any taxes, and which tire not payable in fall within one year, except for interim notes as provided in sections 89-20-30 and 89-20-49 shall be issued or incurred by the district without first submitting a preposition of issuing such bonds or incurring such obligations to the taxpaying elector of the district and being approved be a majority of such electors voting thereon at an election held for that purpose in accordance with this article.

89-20-29. Issuance of temporary bond.--Subject to sections 89-20-19 (1) and 89-20-37, the district may without an election issue temporary bonds, pending preparation of definitive bond or bonds and exchangeable for the definitive bond or bonds when prepared as the board may determine. Each temporary bond shall set forth substantially the same conditions, terms, and provisions as the definitive bond for which it is exchanged. Each holder of any such temporary bond shall have all the rights and remedies which he would have as a holder of the definitive bond or bonds.

89-20-30. Issuance of interim notes.--Subject to sections 89-20-19 (1) and 89-20-37, the district may borrow money and issue interim notes evidencing shortterm loans For the acquisition or improvement land equipment of any mass transportation facility of the district in supplementation of long-term financing and the issuance of bonds, as provided in section 89-20-49.

89-20-31. Pledge of proceeds of taxes and revenues.--The payment of district securities may be secured by the specific pledge of the proceeds of taxes or revenues, or both taxes and net revenues, of the district, as the board may determine. Net revenues pledged for the payment of any securities received by the district shall immediately be subject to the lien of each such pledge without any physical delivery thereof, any filing, or further act, and the lien of each such pledge and the obligation to perform the contractual provisions made in the authorizing resolution or other instrument relating thereto shall have priority over any and all other obligations and liabilities of the district, except as may be otherwise provided in this article or in said resolution or instrument and subject to any prior pledges and liens theretofore created; and the lien of each such pledge shall be valid and binding as against all persons having claims of any kind in tort, contract, or otherwise against the district irrespective of whether such persons have notice thereof.

89-20-32. Ranking among different issues.--Except as otherwise pro-vided in the authorizing resolution of the board, all securities of the same issue or series shall, subject to the prior rights of outstanding securities, claims and other obligations, have a prior lien on the net revenues pledged for the payment of the securities.

89-20-33. Ranking in same issue,--All securities of the same issue or series shall be equally and ratably secured without priority by a lien on the net revenues of the district in accordance with the provisions of this article and the resolution authorizing, or other instrument relating thereto, except to the extent such resolution or other instrument shall otherwise expressly provide.

89-20-34. Payment recital in securities.--District securities issued under this article and constituting special obligations shall recite in substance that the securities and the interest thereon are payable solely from the net revenues of the district pledged to the payment thereof. District securities pledging the full faith and credit of the district for their payment shall so state.

89-20-35. Incontestable recital in securities.--Any resolution authorizing, or other instrument relating thereto under this article, may provide that each security therein designated shall recite that it is issued under authority of this article. Such recital shall conclusively impart full compliance with all the provisions of this article, and all securities issued containing such recital shall be incontestable for any cause whatsoever after their delivery for value.

89-20-36. Limitation upon payment.--The payment of securities shall not be secured by any encumbrance, mortgage, or other pledge of property, of the district, other than net revenues, proceeds of taxes, or any other moneys pledged for the payment of the securities. No property of the district, subject to said exception, shall be liable to be forfeited or taken in payment of the securities.

89-20-37. Limitations upon incurring debt.--The aggregate amount of outstanding securities of the district and any other indebtedness of the district shall not exceed four per cent of the valuation for assessment of the taxable property within the district as shown by the last preceding valuation for assessment for the purposes of taxation.

89-20-38. Security details.--(1) Any district securities authorized to be issued it this article shall bear such date or dates, shall be in suit denomination or denominations, shall mature at such time or times, but in no event exceeding forty years from their date or any shorter limitation provided in this article, shall bear interest at a rate or rates not exceeding seven per cent per annum, which interest may be evidenced by one or two sets of coupons, payable annually or semiannually, except that the first interest payment date appearing to any security may represent interest for any period not in excess of one year, as may be prescribed by resolution or other instrument; and the securities and any coupons shall be payable in such medium of payment at any banking institution or such other place or places within or without the state as determined by the board and the se-curities at the option of the board may be in one or more series, may be made subject to prior redemption in advance of maturity in such order or by lot or otherwise at such time or times without or with the payment of such premium or premiums not exceeding seven per rent of the principal amount of each security so redeemed, as determined by the board.

(2) Any district securities may be issued with privileges for conversion or registration, or both, for payment as to principal or interest, or both, and where interest accruing on the securities is not represented by interest coupons, the securities may provide for the endorsing of payments of interest thereon, and the securities generally shall be issued in such manner, in such form, either coupon or registered, with such recitals, terms, covenants, and conditions, and with such other details, as may be provided by the board in the resolution authorizing the securities, or other instrument appertaining thereto, except as otherwise provided in this article.

(3) Any resolution authorizing the issuance of securities or any other instrument relating thereto may provide for their reissuance in other de-nominations in negotiable or nonnegotiable form and otherwise in such manner and form as the board may determine.

89-20-39. Negotiability.--Subject to the payment provisions specifi-cally provided in this article, any district securities and any interest coupons thereto attached shall be fully negotiable within the meaning of and for all the purpose, of article 8 of chapter 155, C.R.S. 1963, as amended, except as the board may otherwise provide.

89-20-40. Single bonds.--(1) (a) Subject to sections 89-20-19 (1), 89-20-28, and 89-20-37, the board may:

(b) Provide for the initial issuance of one or more securities, in this section called "bond", aggregating the amount of the entire issue, or a designated portion thereof;

(c) Make such provision for installment payments of the principal amount of any such bond as the board may consider desirable;

(d) Provide for the making of any such bond payable to bearer or otherwise, registrable as to principal or as to both principal and interest, and where interest accruing thereon is not rep-resented by interest coupons, for the endorsing of payments of interest on each such bond;

(e) Further make provision in any such proceedings for the man-ner and circumstances in and under which any such bond may in the future, at the request of the holder or owner there-of, be converted into securities of smaller denominations, which securities of smaller denominations may in turn be either coupon bonds or bonds registrable as to principal, or principal and interest, or both, at the option of the holder or owner.

89-20-41. Sale of securities.--(1) Any securities authorized in this article, except for warrants not issued for cash, and except for temporary bonds issued pending preparation of definitive bond or bonds, shall be sold at public or private sale for not less than the principal amount thereof and accrued interest, or at the board's option, below- par at a discount not ex-ceeding seven per cent of the principal amount thereof and at a price which will not result in a net interest cost to the district of more than seven per cent per annum computed to maturity according to standard tables of bond values.

(2) No discount, except as provided in subsection (1) of this section, or commission shall be allowed or paid on or for any security sale to any purchaser or bidder, directly or indirectly.

89-20-42. Application of proceeds.--All moneys received from the issu-ance of any securities authorized in this article shall be used solely for the purpose or purposes for which issued.

89-20-43. Use of unexpended proceeds.--Any unexpended balance of such security proceeds remaining after the completion of the purpose or purposes for which such securities were issued shall be credited immedi-ately to the fund or account created for the payment of the principal of said securities and shall be used therefor, subject to the provisions as to the times and methods for their payment as stated in the securities and the proceedings authorizing or otherwise appertaining to their issuance, or so paid into a reserve therefor.

89-20-44. Covenants in security proceedings.--Any resolution or trust indenture authorizing the issuance of securities or any other instrument relating thereto may contain covenants and other provisions limiting the exercise of powers conferred by this article upon the board in order to secure the payment of such securities, in agreement with the holders and owners of such securities, as the board may determine.

89-20-45. Remedies of security holders.--(1) (a) Subject to contractual limitations binding upon the holders or owners of any issue or series of securities or trustee therefor and subject to any prior or superior rights of others, any holder or owner of securities or trustee therefor shall have the right and power for the equal benefit and protection of all holders and owners of securities similarly situated:

(b) By mandamus or other suit, action, or proceeding at law or in equity to enforce his rights against the district and its board and any of its officers, agents, and employees, and to require and compel the district or its board or any such officers, agents, or employees to perform and carry out its and their duties, obligations, or other commitments under this article and its and their covenants and agreements with the holder or owner of any security;

(c) By action or suit in equity to require the district and its board to account as if they were the trustee of an express trust;

(d) By action or suit in equity to have appointed a receiver, which receiver may enter and take possession of any revenues or any proceeds of taxes, or both, pledged for the payment of the securities. prescribe sufficient fees derived therefrom, and collect, receive, and apply all net revenues or other moneys pledged for the payment of the securities in the same manner as the district itself might do in accordance with the obligations of the district;

(e) By action or suit in equity to enjoin any acts or things which may be unlawful or in violation of the rights of the holder of any security and to bring suit thereupon.

89-20-46. Limitations upon liabilities.--Neither the directors nor any person executing tiny district securities issued under this article shall be liable personally on the securities by reason of the issuance thereof. Securities issued pursuant to this article shall not in any way create or constitute any indebtedness, liability, or obligation of the state or of any political subdivision thereof, except the district, and nothing in this article contained shall be construed to authorize the district to incur any indebtedness on behalf of or in any way to obligate the state or any political subdivision thereof, except the district.

89-20-47. Interest after maturity.--No interest shall accrue on any security authorized in this article after it becomes due and payable if funds for the payment of the principal of and the interest on the security and any prior redemption premium due are available to a paying agent for such payment without default.

89-20-48. Refunding bonds.--(1) Except as otherwise provided in this article, any bonds issued under this article may be refunded without an election, but subject to the provisions of sections 89-20-19 (1), 89-20-28, and 89-20-37, and subject to the provisions concerning their payment and to any other contractual limitations in the proceedings authorizing their issuance or otherwise relating thereto.

(2) Any bond, issued for refunding purposes may either be delivered in exchange for the outstanding bonds authorized to be refunded or may be sold as provided in this article for the sale of other bonds.

(3) No bonds may be refunded under this article unless the holder, thereof voluntarily surrender them for exchange or payment or unless they either mature or are callable for prior redemption under their terms within ten years from the date of issuance of the refunding bonds. Provision shall be made for paying the bonds within said period of time. No maturity

of any bonds refunded may be extended over fifteen years, nor may any interest thereon be increased to any rate exceeding seven per cent per annum. The principal amount of the refunding bonds may exceed the principal amount of the refunded bonds if the aggregate principal and interest costs of the refunding bonds do not exceed such unaccrued costs of the bonds refunded, except the extent any interest on the bonds refunded in ar-rears or about to become due is capitalized with the proceeds of the refund-ing bonds. The principal amount of the refunding bonds may also be less than or the same as the principal amount of the bonds refunded so long as provision is duly and sufficiently made for their payment.

(4) The proceeds of refunding bonds shall either be immediately applied to the retirement of the bonds to he refunded or be placed in escrow or in trust to be applied to the payment of the bonds refunded upon their presentation therefor. Any, proceeds held in escrow or in trust, pending such use, may be invested or reinvested in state or federal securities. Such proceeds and investments in escrow or in trust, together with any interest or other gain to be derived from any such investment, shall be in an amount at all times sufficient as to principal, interest, any prior redemption premium due, and any charges of the escrow agent or trustee payable therefrom, to pay the bonds refunded as they become due at their respective maturities or due at designated prior redemption date or dates upon which the board shall be obligated to call the refunded bonds for prior redemption.

(5) Any refunding bonds shall not be made payable from taxes unless the bonds thereby refunded are payable from taxes, or unless a majority of the taxpaying electors of the district voting on a proposal authorize the issuance by the district of refunding bonds payable from taxes for the purpose of refunding bonds which are not so payable.

(6) Except as otherwise provided in this article, the relevant provisions pertaining to bonds generally shall be equally applicable in the authorization and issuance of refunding bonds, including their terms and security, the bond revolution, trust indenture, taxes, and revenues, and other aspects of the bonds.

89-20-49. Issuance of interim notes.--(1) Whenever a majority of the taxpaying electors of the district voting on a proposal to issue bonds has authorized the district to issue bonds for any purpose authorized in this article, the district may borrow money without any other election in anticipation of taxes or of the proceeds of said bonds and to issue general obligation interim notes to evidence the amount so borrowed, except that the aggregate amount of the interim notes may not exceed the amount so authorized in the election by the qualified taxpaying electors. Any interim notes may mature at such time or time, not exceeding a period of time equal to the estimated time needed to effect the purpose or purposes for which the bonds are authorized to be issued, plus two years, its the board may determine. Except as otherwise provided in this section, interim notes shall be issued as provided in this article for district securities.

(2) Taxes, proceeds of bonds to be thereafter issued or reissued, and bonds issued for the purpose of securing the payment of interim notes, or any combination thereof, may be pledged for the purpose of securing the payment of the interim notes. Any bonds pledged its collateral security for the payment of any interim notes shall mature at such time or times as the board may determine, but In no event exceeding forty years from the date of either any of such bonds or any of such interim notes, whichever date be the earlier. Any such bonds pledged as collateral security shall not be issued in an aggregate principal amount exceeding the aggregate principal

amount of the interim notes or interim notes secured by a pledge of such bonds, nor shall they bear interest at any time which, with any interest accruing at the same time on the interim note or interim notes so secured, exceeds seven per cent per annum.

(3) For the purpose of funding any interim note or interim notes, any bond or bonds pledged as collateral security to secure the payment of such interim note or interim notes, upon their surrender as pledged property, may be reissued without an election, and any bonds not previously issued but authorized to be issued, at an election may be issued for such a funding. Any such bonds shall mature it such time or times as the board may determine, but in no event exceeding forty years from the date of either any of the interim notes so funded or any of the bonds so pledged as collateral se-curity, whichever date be the earlier. Bonds may be issued separately or is-sued in combination in one series or more. Except as otherwise provided in this section any such funding bonds shall be issued as is provided in this article for district securities.

(4) No interim note issued pursuant to the provisions of this sec-tion shall be extended or funded except by the issuance or reissuance of a bond or bonds in compliance with the provi-sions of this section.

89-20-50. Elections.--Where in this article an election of the taxpaying electors of the district shall be permitted or required the election may be held separately at a special election or may be held concurrently with any primary or general election held under the laws of the state; except that no election shall be held at the same time as any regular election of any city, town, or school district within the district.

89-20-51. Election resolution.--(1) (a) The board shall call any elec-tion by resolution adopted at least thirty days prior to the election. Such resolution shall recite:

(b) The objects and purposes of the election for which the indebtedness is proposed to be incurred;

(c) The estimated cost;

(d) How much, if any of said estimated costs is to be defrayed out of any federal grant or money other than that received from indebtedness to be incurred;

(e) The estimated additional annual cost of operation and maintenance of any facility, the acquisition of which said indebtedness, in whole or in part, is to be incurred;

(f) The amount of principal of the indebtedness to be incurred therefor, and the maximum rate of interest to be paid on such indebtedness;

(g) The date upon which such election shall be held and the form of the ballot.

(2) In the case of any election not to be held concurrently with the primary- or general election, the board shall provide for the appointment of sufficient judges and clerks of the election, who shall be taxpaying electors of the district, and in such event shall set their compensation. The election resolution shall also designate the precincts and polling places. Precincts established by any governing body within the district may be consolidated in the election resolution by the board for any election not to be held concurrently with a primary or general election.

(3) If the election shall be held concurrently with a primary or general election held under the laws of the state, the judges of election for such primary or general election shall be designated as the judges of election for the election held pursuant to this article, and they shall receive such additional compensation, if any, as the board shall set by the election resolution.

89-20-52. Conduct of election.--(1) Except as otherwise provided in this article, an election held pursuant hereto shall be opened and conducted in the manner then provided by the laws of the state for the conduct of general elections. Registration pursuant to the general election or any other statutes is not required.

(2) In the event of an election held concurrently with a primary or general election, the county clerk of each of the counties of Adams, Arapahoe, Jefferson, Boulder, Weld, and Douglas, and the election com-mission of the city and county of Denver shall perform for the district election the acts provided by late to be performed by such officials. In the event of an election not held concurrently with a primary or general elec-tion such acts shall be performed by the secretary of the board with the assistance of said county clerks and said election commission. The board, the county clerks and the election commission are authorized to agree among themselves upon the division of such acts and the determination of persons to perform them.

(3) Any taxpaying elector may vote in any election by absent voters ballot tinder the terms and conditions. and in substantially the same man-ner insofar as is practicable, as prescribed in article 14 of chapter 49. C.R.S. 1963. as amended, for general elections, except as specifically modified in this article.

(4) All acts required or permitted to be performed by a county clerk or election commission shall be performed by them respectively in the event of a primary or general election and by the secretary or assistant secretary of the board in the event of any other election, unless the services of the county clerk and election commission are contracted for.

(5) A taxpaying elector may apply for an absent voter's ballot no more than twenty nor less than three days before the election.

(6) No consideration shall be given nor distinction made with reference to any person's political party affiliation or the lack thereof.

(7) The return envelope for the absent voter's ballot shall have printed on its face an affidavit substantially in the following form:

"State of...
County of ....
I, ..., being first duly sworn accord-ing to law, depose and say that my residence and post office address is ....; that I am a person qualified to vote in general elections in the State of Colorado; (that I am a resident of the Regional Transportation District anti an owner of real or personal property within the boundaries of the district, which property is subject to general ad valorem property taxation) or (that I am a person who is obligated to pay general ad valorem property taxes under a contract to purchase real property in the district, at the time of this election). Signature of voter...
Subscribed and sworn to before me this .... day of 19......................

....
(Signature of notary public, county clerk, or other officer authorized to administer oaths)

(SEAL)

...." Title of Office

(8) In any such election at which voting machines are used, the board shall provide paper ballots for absentee voters containing the same question as is to be submitted to the taxpaying electors by the voting machines.

(9) The district may provide for absent voters to cast their absent voters' ballots on voting machines expressly provided for that purpose, if each absent voter indicates by affidavits that he is a taxpaying elector of the district and will be an absent voter, pursuant to section 49-14-10, C.R.S. 1963, and all laws supplemental thereto.

89-20-53.Notice of election.--Notice of such election shall be given by publication. No other notice of an election held under this article need be giver. unless otherwise provided by the board.

89-20-54. Polling places.--All polling places designated by the election resolution shall be within the area included within the district, and if the election shall not be held concurrently with a primary or general election held under the laws of the state, there shall be one polling place in each of the election precincts which are used in the primary and general elections or in each of the consolidated precincts fixed by the board.

89-20-55. Election supplies.--The secretary of the district shall have provided at each polling place ballots or ballot labels, or both, ballot boxes or voting machines, or both, instructions, elector's affidavits, and other material and supplies required for an election by any law. Election officials may require the execution of an affidavit by any person desiring to vote at any election of the district to evidence his qualifications as a taxpaying elector. which affidavit shall be prima facie evidence of the facts stated therein.

89-20-56. Election returns.--(1) In the case of any election held under this article which is not held concurrently with a primary or general election, the election officials shall make their returns directly to the secretary of the district for the board.

(2) In the case of any election held under this article which is consolidated with any primary or general election, the returns thereof shall be made and canvassed at the time and in the manner provided by lace for the canvass of the returns of such primary or general elections. It shall be the duty of such canvassing body to certify promptly and to transmit to the secretary of the district for the board a statement of the result of the vote upon any proposition submitted under this article.

(3) Upon receipt of election returns from election officials or upon re-ceipt of such certificate from any such canvassing body, it shall be the duty of the board to tabulate and declare the results of the election held under this article at any regular or special meeting held not earlier than five days following the date of the election. Except as otherwise provided in this article, any proposal submitted at any election under this article shall not have carried unless the proposal shall have been approved by a majority of the taxpaying electors of the district voting thereon.

89-20-57. District, tax exempted.--The district shall be exempted from any general ad valorem taxes upon any property of the district acquired and used for purposes of this article.

89-20-58. Dissolution of district.--(1) Whenever the board is re-quired to cause the district to be dissolved pursuant to section 89-20-7, the board shall forthwith proceed to defray, to pay and otherwise to liquidate all obligations of the district, including without limitation the expenses of any election.

(2) Any property of the district, other than money, shall be sold or otherwise disposed of as soon as reasonably possible after the board is re-quired to cause the district to be dissolved.

(3) After all obligations have been liquidated or provision has been made therefor, all surplus funds, if any, remaining in the treasury of the district shall be credited to the general fund of each of the counties of Adams, Arapahoe, Jefferson, Boulder, Weld, and Douglas, and the city and county of Denver pro rata according to the value of the taxable property in each of said political subdivisions based upon the last valuation for assess-ment thereof bears to the value of such property in the district.

(4) All records of the district shall be filed with the secretary of state upon the district's dissolution,

(5) A certified true copy of the resolution adopted by the board declar-ing the district dissolved shall be filed by the secretary of the district with each the secretary of state, the county clerk of each the counties of Adams. Arapahoe, Jefferson, Boulder. Weld, and Douglas, and the clerk and re-corder of the city and county of Denver.

(6) The district shall thereupon be dissolved without any other pre-liminaries or further acts.

89-20-59. Freedom from judicial process.--(1) Execution or other judicial process shall not issue against any property autho-rized in this article of the district, nor shall any Judgment against the district be a charge or lien upon its property.

(2) Subsection (1) of this section does not apply to or limit the right of the holder or owner of any district securities, his trustee, or any assignee of all or part of this interest, the federal

government or any public body when it is a party to any contract with the district, and any other obligee under this article to foreclose, to enforce, or to pursue any remedies for the enforcement of any pledge or lien given by the district on the proceeds of any taxes or revenues or both, or any other moneys of the district.

89-20-60. Misdemeanors.--(1) Any person who shall wrongfully damage, injure, or destroy, or in any manner impair the usefulness of any facility. property, structure, improvement, equipment, or other property of the district acquired under the provisions of this article, or shall wrongfully interfere with any officer, agent, or employee of the district in the proper discharge of his duties, shall be guilty of a misdemeanor and upon conviction therefor, shall be punished by a fine in tiny sum not exceeding three hundred dollars or imprisoned in the county jail for a period not to exceed ninety days or by both such fine and imprisonment.

(2) If the district be damaged by any such act, it may also bring a civil action for damages sustained by any such act, and in such proceeding the prevailing party shall also be entitled to reasonable attorneys' fees and costs of court.

89-20-61. Merger, consolidation, or assumption of district.-- Nothing in this article shall be construed to prevent the merger, consolidation, or assumption of the regional transportation district with, into, or by any other district, authority, or political subdivision of the state that may be hereinafter authorized and formed pursuant to the laws and constitution of the state of Colorado, so long as adequate and equitable provisions are made upon merger, consolidation, or assumption for the discharge of all obligations of the district and for the protection of the rights of all holders of securities of the district.

89-20-62. Liberal construction.--This article being necessary to secure and preserve the public health, safety, and general welfare, the rule of strict construction shall have no application to this article, but it shall be liberally construed to effect the purposes and objects for which this article is intended.

Section 2. 80-4-2 (16), Colorado Revised Statutes 1968 (1965 Supp.), is amended to read:

80-4-2. Definitions.--(16) "Authority" shall mean the state of Colorado: any board, commission, agency, or instrumentality thereof; or any DISTRICT, municipality, city and county, or county, or combination there-of, which shall acquire: or operate a mass transportation system as defined in subsection (17) of this section.

Section 3. **Effective date.**--This act shall take effect July 1, 1969.

Section 4. **Safety clause.**--The general assembly hereby finds, determines and declares that this act is necessary for the immediate preservation of the public peace, health, and safety.

Approved: June 7, 1969

Appendix B

AMENDMENT NO. 6 - STATUTE INITIATED BY PETITION

Ballot Title: Shall the Colorado Revised Statues be amended to provide for the election of one director from each director district for a fifteen member board of directors of the Regional Transportation District?

Provisions of the Proposed Statute

The proposed statute would provide for the election of the board of directors of the Denver Regional Transportation District (RTD) for terms beginning in January of 1983. A 15-member board of directors would be elected from individual director districts Board members would be paid an annual salary of $3.000. An outline of election procedures contained in the proposal follows:

—director districts would be apportioned by the governing board of the RTD after each federal census on the basis of population;

—nomination of candidates to appear on the ballot for each director district would be made by petition signed by not less than 100 registered electors in the manner provided lot nominating independent candidates under the general election laws of the state;

—the order of the names of candidates appearing on the ballot would be established by lot;

—at the general election in 1982, eight members of the board of directors would be elected for two-year terms as determined by lot following the apportionment of director districts. Seven members would be elected for four-year terms; and thereafter all members would be elected for four-year terms;

—all board member elections would be held concurrently with the state general election;

—depending on the location of respective director districts, vacancies in director districts wou1C be filled by the governing body of the county or the Mayor of Denver (subject to approval by the city council); and

—recall of board members would be provided in the same manner as for recall of any member of any local improvement and service district (this law requires a recall petition to be signed by not less than ten percent of the qualified electors of the district)

Comments

The Regional Transportation District (RTD) was established by the General Assembly as a political subdivision of the State of Colorado in 1969. Title 32, Article 9, Colorado Revised Statutes of 1973, sets forth the boundaries of the RTD and provides for the appointment of the board of directors of the district The general powers of the district including the taxing authority, and other provisions essential to the operation of the district are established by statute. The district encompasses all of Boulder and Jefferson counties and the City and County of Denver; the urbanized areas of western Adams and Arapahoe counties; and the northeast portion of Douglas County.

The board of directors of the RTD consists of 21 members: two members from Adams, Arapaho-Jefferson, and Boulder counties; one member from Douglas County; ten members from the City and County of Denver; and two at-large directors. Members representing the counties are appointed by the county commissioners; members from Denver are appointed by the Mayor with the approval of the city council; and at-large members are chosen by the other appointed members of the RTD. Appointments to the RTD board by the county commissioners must also be approved by a majority of governing bodies of the municipalities within the respective counties. Terms of members are four years. The RTD statute does not provide specific procedures for removal or recall of a board member.

The organization and operation of the Regional Transportation District is of primary concern to Denver-Area residents, However, in order for any change to occur in state law which governs the operation of the district, legislation must be adopted by the General Assembly or an initiated statute or constitutional amendment must be submitted to all the voters of Colorado for their consideration. Thus, this proposed initiated law will be voted on statewide at the November general election.

Popular Arguments For

1) The governing board of the Regional Transportation District is not directly accountable to the people through an elective process. The organization and structure of the appointed RTD board also diffuses accountability of the board to state and locally elected officials. This weakness of the present governing structure may have contributed in part to recent public criticism of the board's activity.

The Regional Transportation District derives is financial powers from the Colorado General Assembly. State elected officials, however, do not appoint the members of the governing board of the RTD and are not responsible for approval of the budget of the RTD. Local officials make appointments to the governing board of RTD but are not responsible for approval of the budget of the district or for the level of taxation. No elected official and no elected body actually approves the budget of the district. An appointed board is solely responsible for the budget of the RTD. Accountability, whether it involves the expenditure of public funds, operational efficiency, personnel management, or other measure of performance, may be achieved by making elected officials directly responsible for government programs. One way to improve public accountability of the RTD would be through the election of the governing board of the district.

2) Unlike other local issues such as taxation and land use that are subject to a great deal of public scrutiny, appointments to the RTD board are not likely to be critical issues during local elections. Some citizens may even be unaware that local officials are involved in making appointments to the RTD board. The appointive process is deficient in not providing citizens with a mechanism for recall of a member from the governing board of the RTD. Furthermore, the laws governing the RTD do not contain explicit removal provisions for the board of directors. Recent attempts by the General Assembly to change the laws to include removal provisions were unsuccessful. The proposed amendment would allow citizens to actively participate in the management of the RTD by providing both for election and recall of the members of the board of directors.

3) The Regional Transportation District is the fourth largest governmental unit in terms of spending in the state of Colorado with a 1980 budget in excess of 9137 million. Only three units of government are larger in terms of expenditure of public funds- the State of Colorado, the City and County of Denver, and Denver School District No. 1. The enormous expenditure of public funds by the district places the governing board of the RTD in a different position than most other appointed boards and commissions.

In addition to sheer size, the complexity of issues confronting the RTD involve deep philosophical differences among residents of the community. For example, transit systems designed to maximize energy conservation and efficiency may not be of benefit to senior citizens or those members of the metropolitan region who are dependent on conveniently located public transportation. The financial resources of the community maybe hard pressed to support both the development of transportation systems that will be of primary benefit in 1990 or the year 2000 and at the same time substantially improve existing public transit services

It is doubtful that unanimity of opinion could ever be achieved in regard to the myriad of choices available in transportation policy For these reasons, decision-making in the area of public transportation must be responsive to and shared by the public. Candidates for office to an elected RTD board would debate these issues. Direct election of the RTD governing board might help to achieve a public transit policy trial would balance the conflicting needs of residents of the community.

4) The present appointed board of the Regional Transportation District does not provide equal representation in terms of the estimated 1980 population of the district. A total of 19 of the 21 members of the board are appointed by focal units of government. Ten members are from Denver, which means that of the locally appointed members Denver is represented by 52.6 percent of the members. In contrast, Denver's population is an estimated 31.5 percent of the population of the RTD. Jefferson County, with over 23.4 percent of the RTD population, appoints only two of the 19 members or 10.5 percent of the locally appointed board members.

With the exception of Douglas County, which is only partially within the district, the other suburban counties tend to be underrepresented in terms of appointments to the board. Douglas County's RTD population is less than one percent of the district's total estimated population. Douglas County has one board member. The establishment of individual director districts on a population basis as proposed by the amendment would help ensure that board representation would be evenly apportioned throughout the metro area.

5) The 21-member appointed board of the Regional Transportation District may be too large to function efficiently as a governing body. The RTD board has created various subcommittees and delegated responsibilities to an executive committee. The governing boards of other local units of government have far fewer members. Counties are usually governed by three to five members. City councils generally range from seven to 11 members. The proposed amendment would provide nearly a one-third reduction in the size of the RTD board to a more manageable 15-member board.

The proposed reduction in size of the board and the requirement that each board member serve from a director district would mean that one board member would represent any given area in the RTD. Each board member would be familiar with the geography and needs of his area. Thus, residents of any given area in the RTD could contact their representative on the board

Popular Arguments Against

1) In addition to the RTD, there are 33 transit systems in the United States that operate fleets of 200 buses or more. A total of 25 of these transit systems have their own governing boards. Of these 25 boards, only the Alameda Contra Costra Transit District board in Oakland, California is elected. In addition to the aforementioned boards, the Bay Area Rapid Transit District in California, which operates a rail system, also has an elected board. In the organization of large urban transit systems, there has been substantial preference for governance by appointed boards.

Public transit is a key element in community land use planning and traffic control systems. Appointed boards provide direct lines of communication between the transit districts and municipal and county officials. Similarly, the RTD operates buses on local streets and highways and must have a good working relationship with the local governments in the Denver Area. The current appointment of RTD board members by local officials may enhance cooperation among these governmental units. An independently elected board, in which members would be elected from director districts which need not coincide with existing political boundaries, might weaken existing cooperation between the RTD and other local units of government.

2) An effective public transit system is far more important to the densely populated City and County of Denver than to suburban communities. Denver has a higher proportion of residents dependent on public transit and must deal with difficult problems of rush hour traffic congestion of the downtown area. Denver also collects nearly 40 percent of the sales taxes collected by the RTD. The Colorado General Assembly recognized the importance of the central city with regard to the governance of the RTD by providing that ten members of the 21-member board of the RTD would be from Denver. Apportionment of an elected board on the basis of population would mean that Denver's influence on the decisions of the governing board of the Regional Transportation District would be greatly reduced.

3) The 1980 population of the RTD is estimated at 1,655,000. Under the proposal, the average director district would have an estimated population of a little over 110,000 persons. Under the provisions of the proposal, any qualified elector may file for candidacy to the board by filing the signatures of 100 registered electors. This could mean a very large number of candidates running in each district.

The proposal does not provide any procedure for a runoff election and does not utilize a primary election in order to reduce the number of candidates. Voting machines utilized in the general election in the City and County of Denver already are at their capacity. A large number of candidates for an RTD director district seat could make it difficult for candidates to inform voters of their views.

An elective system that might force candidates to seek large campaign donations increases the vulnerability of board members and candidates to be influenced by special interest groups. It would hot be in the public interest to develop an elective system in which it would be possible for a candidate to be elected to the RTD board by only a small percentage of the total votes cast in a director district.

4) The appointive process provides flexibility in the development of a board with a broad-based perspective. The present procedure permits the appointing authorities to nominate persons with a wide variety of skulls in business, finance, labor, government, consumer affairs, land use and transportation planning, etc. Inherent in the power to appoint is the power to remove. Board members of the RTD have resigned when requested by appointing authorities.

A prime requisite for an elective policy-making board is its capacity to consider public transit issues in terms of an entire system. The RTD is supported from both user charges and tax revenues. If transit services are to be developed in a cost effective manner, policy makers must make decisions based on the impact to the entire district. The present appointive structure of the RTD board permits members to view decisions from a regional perspective. A board comprised of individuals elected from director districts would be subject to considerable pressure from the parochial interests of their respective constituencies to the detriment of an integrated and comprehensive public transit system.

5) The proposed amendment could mean that the present board of the Regional Transportation District would become a "lame duck" board at a critical time in the development of tran-

sit systems in the Denver Metropolitan Area. Voters in the RTD will be considering whether to authorize funding for the construction of a light rail system at the November general election. Under this proposal, the present board members and new members appointed in July of 1981 would serve until January of 1983. Thus for nearly two years, the appointed board would be in office at a time in which there could be considerable negotiation with transit planning consultants, contractors, and local governments. There could be great reluctance among such individuals and organizations to make commitments to a lame duck governing board.

Rocky Mountain News

MAC on the move
Sun. July 5, 1992

Light-rail project shows where there's a will, there's a way

By Jack McCroskey

After a quarter century of broken promises false starts and political misadventure light rail is coming to metropolitan Denver. Finally . . . and without new taxes.

Called the Metro Area Connection (MAC), RTD's 5.3 mile light-rail line is slated to run from 30th Avenue at Downing through Five Points and downtown Denver to the Colorado Convention Center and Auraria Campus. From there, along railroad right-of-way, it will go to the Gates Rubber Co. at Interstate 25 and Broadway.

What is light rail? It's an up-to-date, smooth-riding, version of the electric trolley. It carries more passengers faster and more dependably than buses. It doesn't pollute the neighborhoods it travels through. It is quiet; it doesn't rattle nearby building and houses.

But it is difficult to put into words the manifold differences between light rail and internal-combustion motor buses—differences in comfort, appearance and ambiance This difficulty is one reason some citizens remain skeptical about light rail. Will it attract enough passengers? Will it really work?

We believe that it will—as is attested to by the experience of other North American cities from Portland to Calgary to San Diego. But to settle the issue here in Denver, we need it demonstration line. We need MAC.

If citizens decide they don't particularly care for the demon-stration, MAC will serve as a salutary stand-alone line, reducing congestion and pollution in downtown Denver while providing daily transportation for thousands. But if citizens opt for more rail, as seems likely, then MAC can extend out into a regional system. It is actually the first leg of every line in the region.

The eight corridors identified on the accompanying map are pretty much the same corridors RTD has been studying and plan-ning to build for 25 years. considerable work has been done on every corridor. For example:

On the North Corridor (No. 2 on the map), construction is already under way on bus-carpool lanes between downtown and U.S. 36; these lanes are separated from general traffic and can be upgraded to rail in the future. On the Southwest Corridor (No. 5), using a $1.8 million federal grant RTD is conducting what transit officials call an "alternatives analysis," which constitutes the crucially important first step toward selecting a technology, and in gaining federal funds for construction. In the Northeast Corridor (No. 8), Denver, with RTD's support, is looking at com-muter rail possibilities.

But the most persistent questions we hear aren't about plans for a regional system. Nor are they about MAC's possible success or failure. Most people, m News columnist Gene Amole's words, want a chance to "kick the tires and drive it around the block." The besetting questions are these:

1) Why don't you build a line to the Denver Tech Center or to the new airport? RTD simply doesn't have the money at the present time to build l5 miles to the Tech Center or 22 miles to the new airport.

2) Why not build MAC somewhere else? The map shows that MAC stands at the center of the regional system. It is the heart of the system. Putting the first 5.3 miles somewhere else wouldn't make good sense.

Here are 10 additional questions we have been asked many tunes during the more than 300 public meetings held during the past three years:

3) Five miles seems pretty short. What public purposes will be promoted? MAC serves a much-needed demonstration line, giving metro citizens a first-hand opportunity to judge for themselves whether they want more Together with the bus-carpool lanes along 1-25, MAC will let us measure the comparative efficiency and attractiveness of the two premier modes of rapid transit If the decision goes against additional light rail, MAC will remain as a cost-effective, pollution and aggravation reducing part of our overall transportation system.

4) Will MAC reduce pollution? Yes. Congestion? Yes. MAC will allow RTD to dispense with 530 bus trips daily—a direct savings to RTD of $2.25 million annually. As the system builds out, more bus trips can be eliminated.

5) Will there be park-n-rides along the line? Yes.

6) When will construction begin? We start this summer with all reasonable consideration given to minimizing traffic and shopping inconvenience. It will be ready to ride in the summer of 1994.

7) How much will a ride cost? The same as local buses. with free transfers between rail and bus lines.

8) What are the construction costs? Including eleven 157—passenger cars and a maintenance facility, gross costs will amount to $100 million. Net costs, which are gross cost, minus the present value of bus savings, will run to $70 million. No new taxes are necessary.

9) How do light-rail operating costs compare with bus operating costs? Most cities operating both buses and light rail report that the operating costs for rail are lower than the costs for buses—in other words, rail subsidies generally run below bus subsidies.

10) How have things worked out in other cities? Does ridership meet expectations? A frequently reprinted report written in 1989 for the U.S. Department of Transportation has generated all manner of hostility and bias toward light rail. Committing sins of both omission and commission, the report omits all reference to the monumental government subsidies going to petroleum powered vehicles. Further, it doesn't include in its overall conclusions the results from hugely successful light-rail systems such as the one in San Diego.

11) Why build a system similar to the old trolley system that was torn out so long ago? America pioneered electric propulsion. and cities across the country were enjoying highly civilized trolley and streetcar transit at a time when London, Berlin and Tokyo were still mired in horse manure. All of which is one reason why June 3, 1950, the last day streetcars plied Denver streets, is remembered by many long-time residents as a day for mourning—a day exemplifying the saying that "not all change is progress." Such change happened across the country, give or take a few years, and was owing in large part to three developments:

One, governments gave very large subsidies to petroleum-powered vehicles. Two. governments taxed street railways at high rates and in highly discriminatory ways. Three, General Motors and Standard Oil joined in a series of predatory attacks against streetcars.

No responsible observer would deny that automobiles were destined to play a leading role in metropolitan transportation, especially under the spur of post-World War II prosperity and suburbanization. Nonetheless, if government had followed neutral policies rather than policies prejudicial to streetcars, our urban landscape would look very different than it looks today.

12) What comes after MAC? No one can say for sure. Here, however, are three possibilities:

A. Citizens find they don't particularly like light rail MAC stays on as a stand-alone line Probability? Low

B. Citizens welcome light rail with open arms, finding n an attractive, congestion-reducing and cost-effective way to promote mobility. They vote tax increases to build the entire regional system as quickly as possible. Probability? Middling.

C. Citizens like light rail very much, but facing shaky economic conditions decline to vote for more taxes—RTD moves to expand the system in measured ways, using federal funds, bus savings and various tax increments.

We aren't disposed to argue that a gradual build is the most probable future, but we insist that systems can start small and move forward prudently. Where there's a will, in matters of public transportation, there is also a way.

Jack McCroskey represents District A and is chairman of the board of the Regional Transportation District.

Appendix D

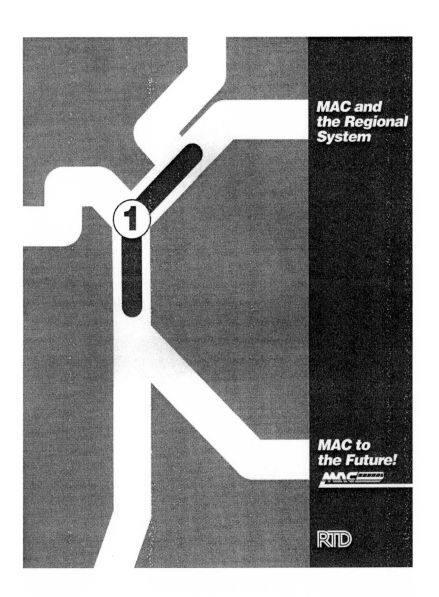

MAC and
the Regional
System

MAC to
the Future!

RTD

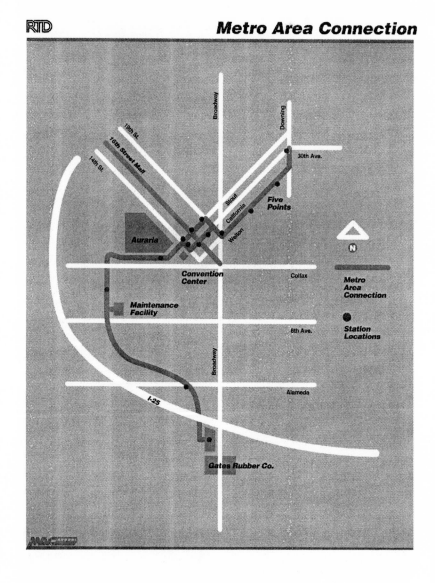

Facts on the Regional System

System Overview

Rapid transit planning at RTD has gone on since RTD's creation in 1969. Over the years, eight transit corridors have been identified as the areas best suited for rapid transit. Various rapid transit planning and construction activities have taken place in each corridor.

Central ❶

The Central Corridor is the site of the Metro Area Connection (MAC) light rail project. This corridor will provide the spine, or center, segment of the entire rapid transit system. By building this segment first, RTD is able to lower the cost of building other corridors as well as provide a collection/distribution line for the entire system.

North ❷

The North Corridor extends along North I-25 between downtown and 120th Avenue. The "Downtown Express", currently under construction between downtown and 58th Avenue, will be two lanes in the center of I-25 that are barrier-separated from general traffic, with limited access points. These lanes will be for the exclusive use of buses and carpools, and will run inbound in the morning rush hour and outbound in the evening. A second phase will extend these exclusive lanes to 120th Avenue. These lanes can be upgraded to rail transit in the future.

Northwest ❸

The Northwest Corridor extends from I-25 to Boulder along U.S. 36. Currently, RTD has a bus-only lane (inbound only) that runs between Lowell Boulevard and I-25. In 1992 this lane will be extended to Sheridan Boulevard. When the Downtown Express along North I-25 is complete, buses using U.S. 36 will have a direct entry to the Bus/carpool lanes. Bus patrons are currently saving a significant amount of travel time per day.

West ❹

The West Corridor extends from the Auraria MAC station west along 13th Avenue to the Federal Center. RTD purchased the Associated Railroad line that parallels 13th Avenue from the Platte River to Quail Street. Negotiations are underway with the General Service Administration to acquire the rail right-of-way from Quail Street to the Federal Center. No funding is in place for this corridor.

Southwest ❺

The Southwest Corridor extends south from the south end of the MAC at I-25 and Broadway, paralleling South Santa Fe Drive, through the Cities of Englewood and Littleton to C-470. The corridor has been identified as the region's "priority corridor" by both RTD and the Denver Regional Counsel of Governments. When the Colorado Department of Transportation (CDOT) decided to widen Santa Fe it had to move the existing railroad tracks to the east, and improve numerous intersections along Santa Fe. In return for RTD's participation in the intersection improvements, CDOT has reserved space between the relocated railroads and Santa Fe for rapid transit. In April of 1992 the Federal Transit Administration (FTA), approved a grant application by RTD to proceed with an Alternatives Analysis. This study is required in order to determine the alignment, station placement and transit technology preferred for this corridor. The Southwest Corridor Alternatives Analysis will also result in the production of a Draft Environmental Impact Statement.

Southeast ❻

The Southeast Corridor extends from the south end of the MAC at I-25 and Broadway to the Denver Tech Center generally along I-25. RTD owns right-of-way along Buchtel Boulevard which could potentially be used for rapid transit in this corridor. CDOT is currently including a space for future transit in all of the bridge widening they do along south I-25. No funding is in place for this corridor.

Aurora South ❼

The Aurora South Corridor runs along I-225 between I-70 and I-25. Right-of-way is being preserved in the center of the highway as bridges are reconstructed. No funding is in place for this corridor.

Northeast (Airport) ❽

The Northeast Corridor begins where the MAC ends, at 30th Avenue and Downing, and will proceed northeast to both Stapleton and the new Denver International Airport. The City of Denver has conducted a "feasibility analysis" that looks at the possibility of "commuter rail" from Denver Union Terminal to the new airport. Commuter rail utilizes diesel trains on existing tracks. No funding is in place for this corridor.

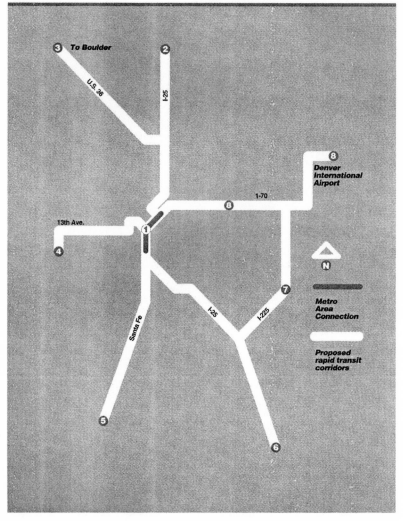

RTD

Facts on MAC

System Overview

RTD's first light rail system, the Metro Area Connection (MAC), will run from 30th Avenue and Downing through the Five Points business district and downtown Denver, by the Auraria campus and then along railroad right-of-way to I-25 and Broadway.

This system will be funded entirely by RTD; no tax increase and no federal dollars will be necessary. The northern part of the MAC, between Downing and Auraria will be funded with an existing use tax. The southern part of the line, between Auraria and I-25/Broadway, will be financed by the savings realized by taking approximately 500 bus trips a day off city streets.

The MAC will be 5.3 miles long and is projected to carry 13,000 riders a day. A bus transfer station and a small park-n-Ride are planned at 30th/Downing. At I-25/ Broadway, Express, Regional and some Local bus passengers coming from the south will transfer to the MAC. Local bus service along Broadway and Lincoln will be increased.

This first line, the spine of the planned regional rapid transit system, will demonstrate what light rail is and the benefits it can provide. Opening day is scheduled for 1994.

System Benefits

- Provides a starter line for the regional system.
- Becomes a demonstration of what light rail is, does and looks like.
- Removes more than 500 bus trips/day from downtown city streets.
- Reduces air pollution & traffic congestion.
- Provides an opportunity for economic development in commercial areas that surround the proposed system.
- Increases chances for federal funds for future projects.
- Demonstrates Denver's commitment to rapid transit.

System Characteristics

- 5.3-mile length
- Up to 55 mph speeds
- Frequency of trains
  - every 5 minutes (rush hour)
  - every 10 minutes (non-rush hours)
- Fully handicapped-accessible

- Spine of regional system
- Proven off-the-shelf technology
  - Overhead electrical power
  - Ground-level light rail
- Simple stations

System Costs/Ridership

- Gross Capital Costs ....$103 million
- Net Capital Costs (Gross Cost minus bus operating savings) ....$68-70 million
  - Includes:
    - Maintenance Facility ....$12.1 million
    - 11 Vehicles ....$18.9 million

- Operating & Maintenance Costs ....$3.7 million/year

- Opening Day Ridership 13,000/day

1061 MAC 6/92

APPENDIX E

COLORADO COURT OF APPEALS

Court of Appeals No. 00CA1778
City and County of Denver District Court No. 99CV7676
Honorable Paul A. Markson, Jr., Judge

Gloria Holliday, individually and as a member of the board of directors of the Regional Transportation District; and Jack McCroskey, individually and as a member of the board of directors of the Regional Transportation District,

Plaintiffs-Appellants,

v.

Regional Transportation District; Robert L. Tonsing, individually and as chairman of the board of directors of the Regional Transportation District; and Brenda Bergman, individually and as executive assistant to the board of directors of the Regional Transportation District,

Defendants-Appellees.

JUDGMENT REVERSED AND CASE
REMANDED WITH DIRECTIONS

Division V
Opinion by JUDGE CASEBOLT
Vogt and Criswell*, JJ., concur

September 27, 2001

Ben Klein, Denver, Colorado, for Plaintiffs-Appellants

Marla L. Lien, Associate Counsel, Regional Transportation District, Denver, Colorado, for Defendants-Appellees

*Sitting by assignment of the Chief Justice under provisions of Colo. Const. art. VI, § 5(3), and § 24-51-1105, C.R.S. 2001.

In this action under 42 U.S.C. § 1983 asserting violations of the First Amendment, plaintiffs, Gloria Holliday and Jack McCroskey, appeal the judgment dismissing their claims against defendants, Robert L. Tonsing, Brenda Bergman, and the Regional Transportation District (RTD). We reverse and remand for further proceedings.

Except as indicated, the following facts are either undisputed or are taken from plaintiffs' uncontroverted affidavits.

RTD is a political subdivision of the state that is authorized to develop, maintain, and operate a mass transportation system. Holliday is a current member of the RTD board of directors, and until January 1, 2001, McCroskey was also a board member. Tonsing served as the chair of the board of directors until January 2000, and Bergman is the board executive assistant responsible for the supervision of RTD administrative staff.

Members of the board, also known as district directors, are elected by geographic district. District directors maintain offices at RTD headquarters in Denver and have access to RTD administrative resources, including secretarial staff.

Among the functions traditionally carried out by RTD

administrative staff is the typing and mailing of letters written by board members. Before the events giving rise to this case, district directors typically used RTD administrative staff to send letters communicating with other government officials and their constituents on RTD policy matters. The content of these communications typically included praise or criticism of RTD policy, staff, officers, and directors. This correspondence was not traditionally subject to review for content.

Acting in the wake of a particular instance in which administrative staff were used to communicate criticisms of RTD staff and former directors to the news media, Tonsing issued a memo to all district directors concerning the use of RTD resources. Tonsing's memo stated a new policy:

> RTD board resources, including staff assistance and materials, are available in support of directors' activities that clearly have to do with carrying out the agency's responsibilities under state law, and RTD by-laws and directives. Accordingly, I have directed the board staff not to provide such support when any reasonable person would conclude that other agendas (some of which might in fact hinder the RTD mission) are at work.

The memo stated that Tonsing himself would make the determination regarding the use of staff in "borderline" cases.

After the resource policy was announced, plaintiffs continued to draft and submit their correspondence for typing by RTD administrative staff. On at least sixteen occasions, either Tonsing or Bergman returned plaintiffs' correspondence to them untyped. The draft correspondence for which plaintiffs were not given RTD staff assistance included letters to state officials and at least one letter to the editor of a local newspaper. Almost all of the letters as drafted showed copies going to members of local Denver media outlets.

The subjects of the untyped letters varied but all related to RTD matters. The letters included criticism of RTD policies with regard to light rail; allegations of conflict of interest against district directors; allegations of waste, mismanagement, electioneering, and cronyism against RTD officers; calls for termination of officers; and discussion of the issues surrounding an RTD bond ballot measure.

When returning the untyped draft correspondence, Bergman and Tonsing often included a note indicating the reason for the rejection of the correspondence. The reasons noted for rejection included that the correspondence contained personal attacks, name calling, unfounded accusations, slander, unsubstantiated claims, and statements that were contrary to RTD policy.

All of plaintiffs' letters rejected by Tonsing and Bergman were ultimately distributed by other means. Several of the letters, and the application of the resource policy itself, became the subject of local newspaper stories.

In the wake of the institution of the resource policy, plaintiffs alleged that other directors' correspondence was not rejected or scrutinized. In a memo to the board, Tonsing denied that other directors' correspondence was not scrutinized and insisted that only plaintiffs, and specifically plaintiff McCroskey, had submitted correspondence that violated the terms of the resource policy.

Plaintiffs communicated their objections concerning the policy to both Tonsing and Bergman. According to plaintiffs' affidavits, both Tonsing and Bergman stated in response that they would not allow dissemination of correspondence that was unfavorable to RTD, and that the purpose of the policy was to ensure that plaintiffs could not disseminate their criticisms, but could only communicate information that was favorable to RTD. Tonsing also stated that he would do anything within his power to prevent plaintiffs from communicating information to their constituents that was contrary to RTD board policy.

Plaintiffs then initiated this proceeding, alleging violations of their First Amendment rights and their rights under article II, § 10 of the Colorado Constitution. Tonsing and RTD filed a motion for summary judgment, claiming that the policy did not constitute an infringement of plaintiffs' rights. Defendants Bergman and RTD separately filed a motion to dismiss on the basis that Bergman was not in a policymaking position and only acted on Tonsing's instructions.

The trial court granted both motions and ruled that the remaining motions, including a motion to add a defendant, were moot. Plaintiffs appeal the resulting judgment of dismissal.

I.

Plaintiffs contend that the trial court erred in granting summary judgment on their claims. They assert that, drawing all inferences from the undisputed facts in their favor, there is sufficient evidence to warrant a trial on their claim that defendants violated their First Amendment rights and that, in any event, material issues of fact remain that preclude summary judgment. We agree in part.

We review a summary judgment de novo. *Aspen Wilderness Workshop, Inc. v. Colo. Water Conservation Bd.*, 901 P.2d 1251 (Colo. 1995).

De novo review is also appropriate when the issues raised touch on First Amendment concerns. In such cases, an appellate court must make an independent review of the whole record to ensure that the judgment rendered does not intrude on the right of free speech. *Rankin v. McPherson*, 483 U.S. 378, 107 S.Ct. 2891, 97 L.Ed.2d 315 (1987); *Mesa v. White*, 197 F.3d 1041 (10th Cir. 1999); *Lewis v. Colo. Rockies Baseball Club*, 941 P.2d 266 (Colo. 1997).

Summary judgment is appropriate only if the pleadings and supporting documents demonstrate that there is no genuine issue as to any material fact and that the moving party is entitled to judgment as a matter of law. The burden is on the moving party to establish that no genuine issue of fact exists, and any doubts in this regard must be resolved against that party. The nonmoving party is entitled to the benefit of all favorable inferences that may reasonably be drawn from the undisputed facts. *Aspen Wilderness Workshop, Inc. v. Colo. Water Conservation Bd., supra.*

We note initially that article II, § 10 of the Colorado Constitution provides greater protection for freedom of speech than does the First Amendment. *Lewis v. Colo. Rockies Baseball Club, supra.* Nevertheless, neither party argues that a conceptual framework different from First Amendment analysis governs this case when analyzed with respect to the Colorado Constitution. Instead, the parties have analyzed this case in the context of the protections accorded by the First Amendment. The supreme court has previously found it unnecessary to consider the more expansive protections of the Colorado Constitution where federal jurisprudence has established a framework for considering the restriction of speech on public property, see *Lewis v. Colo. Rockies Baseball Club, supra,* and we conclude likewise here. Accordingly, our analysis proceeds solely under the First Amendment.

Under federal constitutional jurisprudence, we follow a three-step approach to determine whether the policy at issue constitutes an impermissible intrusion upon First Amendment protections. First, we consider whether the claim involves protected speech and whether the government is involved in its abridgment. *See Lewis v. Colo. Rockies Baseball Club, supra.*

Second, if the speech is subject to protection, we must determine the nature of the forum involved, because the extent to which the government may limit access depends on whether the forum is public or nonpublic. Because a principal purpose of a traditional public forum is the free exchange of ideas, speakers may be excluded from a public forum only if the exclusion is necessary to serve a compelling state interest and the exclusion is narrowly drawn to achieve that interest. Similarly, when the government has intentionally designated a place or means of communication as a public forum, speakers cannot be excluded without a compelling governmental interest. Access to a nonpublic forum, however, can be restricted as long as the restrictions are reasonable and are not an effort to suppress expression merely because public officials oppose the speaker's view. *Cornelius v. NAACP Legal Def. & Educ. Fund*, 473 U.S. 788, 105 S.Ct. 3439, 87 L.Ed.2d 567 (1985).

Third, we determine whether the justification for exclusion from the forum satisfies the requisite standard. *Cornelius v. NAACP Legal Def. & Educ. Fund, supra; Perry Educ. Ass'n v. Perry Local Educators' Ass'n*, 460 U.S. 37, 103 S.Ct. 948, 74 L.Ed.2d 794 (1983); *Mesa v. White, supra; Lewis v. Colo. Rockies Baseball Club, supra; see also Int'l Soc'y for Krishna Consciousness v. Lee*, 505 U.S. 672, 112 S.Ct. 2701, 120 L.Ed.2d 541 (1992).

A.

Concerning the first step, plaintiffs' letters here constitute protected speech. The letters address matters of public concern, including allegations of conflicts of interest, waste, mismanagement, and cronyism in the operation of a state agency. The letters also contain criticism of agency policy and the actions of agency officials. This speech is not only protected, but is entitled to the greatest protection within the framework of the First Amendment as speech by elected officials that criticizes public policy. *See Bond v. Floyd*, 385 U.S. 116, 87 S.Ct. 339, 17 L.Ed.2d 235 (1966). Moreover, because RTD acknowledges it is a government agency, it is the "government" that is regulating plaintiffs' speech.

B.

Turning to the second step, we analyze the nature of the governmental property or process to which plaintiffs seek access and conclude that it is not a public forum.

The government need not permit all forms of speech on property or using processes that it owns and controls. To the contrary, the government, no less than a private property owner, has the power to preserve governmental property and processes to the uses for which they are lawfully dedicated. *Cornelius v. NAACP Legal Def. & Educ. Fund, supra, Perry Educ. Ass'n v. Perry Local Educators' Ass'n, supra.*

The typical public forum is property, such as public streets and parks, that traditionally has been used by the public for purposes of assembly and expression, and where such expression has always been subject to only minimal restriction. The limited or designated public forum is a location that the government has opened to the public for expression. Examples may include university meeting facilities and school grounds, if opened for use by the public. The nonpublic forum is public property that is not by tradition or designation a forum for public communication. *Perry Educ. Ass'n v. Perry Local Educators' Ass'n, supra.*

In analyzing the forum, we consider not only the nature of the tangible governmental property or process to which access is sought, but also the type of access that is sought. *Cornelius v. NAACP Legal Def. & Educ. Fund, supra.* In *Perry*, for instance, the "forum" was a school interoffice mail system to which a teachers union sought access. In *Cornelius*, the forum was a federal employee charity drive in which various advocacy groups wanted to participate.

Here, the forum is best described not as the physical location of RTD headquarters, but rather as the administrative resources at RTD headquarters, including secretarial staff and funds involved in the typing and mailing of directors' communications.

We conclude that this forum is nonpublic in nature because neither the state nor RTD has offered the use of RTD resources to the public for expressive purposes. Further, the business of the RTD is to provide mass transportation, not to provide a public forum.

This conclusion is not altered by the fact that RTD resources are used by directors, including plaintiffs, as a means for communicating with the public. In *Cornelius*, advocacy groups claiming a right to participate in a federal employee charity drive relied on the fact that groups already involved in the drive were given the opportunity to include descriptions of their purposes and functions in the materials distributed to employees. This communication, the plaintiffs argued, transformed the charity drive into a forum for expression by these groups. The Court disagreed, concluding that the government did not create the charity drive as a forum for individual expression, but as a vehicle to encourage federal employees to make voluntary contributions to charity. The fact that expressive activity occurred incidentally did not alter the nonpublic nature of the forum. *Cornelius v. NAACP Legal Def. & Educ. Fund, supra.*

Similarly, here, RTD resources exist to support the functions of the agency, not to create a forum for plaintiffs' expression. The fact that plaintiffs and other directors have used RTD resources as a means of communication with the public does not change the nature of the forum.

C.

Turning to the third step, although the government may regulate speech in a nonpublic forum to reserve the forum for its intended purposes, communicative or otherwise, we must determine whether the distinctions drawn are both reasonable and viewpoint neutral. *See Perry Educ. Ass'n v. Perry Local Educators' Ass'n, supra.* These requirements are conjunctive, not disjunctive. The existence of reasonable grounds for limiting access to a nonpublic forum will not save a regulation or policy that is in reality a façade for viewpoint-based discrimination. *Cornelius v. NAACP Legal Def. & Educ. Fund, supra.* We conclude that there are genuine issues of material fact here as to whether the distinctions drawn by defendants are viewpoint neutral.

Discrimination against speech because of its message is presumed to be unconstitutional. It is axiomatic that the government may not regulate speech based on its substantive content or the message it conveys. *Rosenberger v. Rector & Visitors of Univ. of Va.,* 515 U.S. 819, 828, 115 S.Ct. 2510, 2516, 132 L.Ed.2d 700, 714 (1995).

With narrow exceptions in areas such as obscenity, viewpoint discrimination is almost universally condemned and rarely passes constitutional scrutiny. *Mesa v. White, supra*. The Supreme Court, applying the test of reasonableness and viewpoint neutrality, has struck down government restrictions that discriminated against a religious viewpoint. *Good News Club v. Milford Cent. Sch.*, ___ U.S. ___, 121 S.Ct. 2093, 150 L.Ed.2d 151 (2001); *Rosenberger v. Rector & Visitors of Univ. of Va., supra*.

In testing a policy for viewpoint discrimination, we may consider its application as well as the language of the policy on its face. *Mesa v. White, supra* (concluding that rule of procedure used to bar speaker at county commission meeting was a pretext for viewpoint discrimination); *Tucker v. Cal. Dep't of Educ.*, 97 F.3d 1204 (9th Cir. 1996) (summary judgment inappropriate where facially neutral restrictions may be applied to discriminate on basis of viewpoint).

Here, plaintiffs assert that the resource policy has been applied only to them and the viewpoints they espouse, a charge that defendant Tonsing denies. The notations transmitted by Bergman and Tonsing appear to support plaintiffs' assertions that the policy was applied on the basis of disagreement with plaintiffs' views. None of these notations refers to the need to preserve resources, which was the facial reason given for establishment of the policy. Instead, the notations dispute the message contained in the correspondence. Rejections on the basis that there are "unsubstantiated claims" or "unfounded allegations" evidence that the person reviewing the letter disagrees with the stance taken by the author.

Indeed, the face of the policy itself is not viewpoint neutral. Its specific language precludes support for "other agendas" that "might hinder" RTD's work.

In addition, defendants do not contest plaintiffs' assertions that Tonsing and Bergman admitted that the policy as adopted is a pretext for silencing plaintiffs' criticisms of RTD.

All of this evidence taken together raises issues of material fact concerning whether the resource policy as applied is an instance of pure viewpoint discrimination that the First Amendment cannot abide.

While viewpoint discrimination is always subject to the most stringent review, our concern is even greater given the circumstances of this case. Plaintiffs here were restrained in their effort to communicate criticism of governmental actions. "'Whatever differences may exist about interpretations of the First Amendment, there is practically universal agreement that a major purpose of that Amendment was to protect the free discussion of governmental affairs.' 'For speech concerning public affairs is more than self-expression; it is the essence of self-government.'" *Burson v. Freeman,* 504 U.S. 191, 196, 112 S.Ct. 1846, 1850, 119 L.Ed.2d 5, 12 (1992)(citation omitted; quoting *Mills v. Alabama,* 384 U.S. 214, 218, 86 S.Ct. 1434, 1437, 16 L.Ed.2d 484, 488 (1966), and *Garrison v. Louisiana,* 379 U.S. 64, 74-75, 85 S.Ct. 209, 216, 13 L.Ed.2d 125, 133 (1964)).

Plaintiffs' status as elected officials heightens our concern, for with that status they are entitled to receive the "widest latitude to express their views on issues of policy." *Bond v. Floyd, supra,* 385 U.S. at 136, 87 S.Ct. at 349, 17 L.Ed.2d at 247.

In *Bond,* the Supreme Court considered the claim of a state legislator that he had been denied the opportunity to take the oath of office and be seated as a member of the legislature because of statements he made in opposition to the Vietnam war. The state argued that the statements demonstrated a lack of loyalty to the state and the nation that precluded the plaintiff from taking the oath of office. The Court rejected that argument and affirmed the primacy of political speech by elected officials in the hierarchy of First Amendment concerns, stating: "Legislators have an obligation to take positions on controversial political questions so that their constituents can be fully informed by them, and be better able to assess their qualifications for office; also so they may be represented in governmental debates by the person they have elected to represent them." *Bond v. Floyd, supra*, 385 U.S. at 136-37, 87 S.Ct. at 349-50, 17 L.Ed.2d at 248.

Plaintiffs, like the state legislator in *Bond*, are elected to represent a constituency defined by districting, and in that representative capacity they are obligated to debate and to vote on matters affecting public policy. See § 32-9-109.5, C.R.S. 2001.

Our view is buttressed by *Ridgeway v. Kiowa School District* C-2, 794 P.2d 1020 (Colo. App. 1989), a case with important similarities to this one. There, a division of this court reversed the summary judgment that had been granted in favor of the defendant school district and against the teacher-plaintiff claiming a violation of First Amendment rights. The division concluded that summary judgment was inappropriate in the face of a claim that the district, in issuing a formal reprimand to the teacher, had been motivated by a desire to punish the teacher for publishing remarks that were critical of the district. The division noted that summary judgment is usually inappropriate in cases dealing with potentially unconstitutional motivations. Because evidence concerning motive is almost always subject to a variety of conflicting interpretations, a full trial on the merits is normally the only way to separate permissible motivations from those that merely mask unconstitutional actions.

Similarly, here, the facts implicate the motivations of defendants in promulgating and applying the resource policy.

Accordingly, because plaintiffs' factual assertions in their affidavits coupled with defendants' denials raise substantial issues of material fact, the summary judgment in defendants' favor cannot stand.

II.

Defendants nevertheless argue that there was no actual infringement of plaintiffs' First Amendment rights because plaintiffs did not have a right in the first instance to use government resources to subsidize their own expression. Furthermore, they assert, the restriction involved, which merely withheld secretarial support and mailing costs, was so slight as to be *de minimis*.

Defendants also point out that plaintiffs had reasonable alternative means of communicating, which they were not prevented from using. And, the fact that plaintiffs' criticisms were the subject of newspaper articles shows that plaintiffs were successful in communicating their message without the use of RTD resources. We are not persuaded.

It is true that the government is not required to subsidize the exercise of fundamental rights, including the right to free expression. However, having made the determination to fund certain speech, the government may not discriminate among speakers based on viewpoint. *Rosenberger v. Rector & Visitors of Univ. of Va., supra.*

In *Rosenberger*, the Supreme Court ruled in favor of a religious student group that was denied university funding to print its newsletter while such funding was made available to other groups with secular viewpoints. Ruling separately that funding this religious group would not violate the establishment clause of the First Amendment, the Court concluded that once the university offered funding to student groups wishing to convey a message, the university could not silence the expression of selected viewpoints. *Rosenberger v. Rector & Visitors of Univ. of Va., supra.*

Here, once the RTD provided funding and resources to directors to communicate with their constituents and others, it could not thereafter selectively foreclose the dissemination of other viewpoints regarding RTD business.

Moreover, regulation of speech that does not amount to a total prohibition may nevertheless impermissibly infringe the freedom of speech. The Supreme Court has particularly noted the deterrent or chilling effect of government restrictions that fall short of direct prohibitions on speech. *See United States v. Playboy Entm't Group, Inc.*, 529 U.S. 803, 120 S.Ct. 1878, 146 L.Ed.2d 865 (2000).

For example, the Court has held that a parade permit fee that varied based on the content of the speech of the applicant was unconstitutional, and that it was of no moment that the fee in question could be nominal. "A tax based on the content of speech does not become more constitutional because it is a small tax." *Forsyth County v. Nationalist Movement*, 505 U.S. 123, 136, 112 S.Ct. 2395, 2405, 120 L.Ed.2d 101, 115 (1992).

In *Perry Education Ass'n, supra,* the Court applied its forum analysis to the regulation at issue despite the fact that the regulation could be characterized as *de minimis,* because the regulation only denied a teachers union access to school interoffice mail facilities. It was undisputed that the union was seeking a right to use government resources to facilitate private communication. It was also uncontested that alternative modes, such as the regular mail, existed and were used by the union for communication. The Court, while taking these factors into account in finding the regulation at issue reasonable for a nonpublic forum, considered the union's claims on the merits, and noted that such a restriction would not be acceptable if it discriminated on the basis of the speaker's viewpoint.

Here, applying the *Perry* proscription against viewpoint discrimination, the fact that defendants are restricting plaintiffs' speech in a way that does not amount to total prohibition and that alternative means of communication remain, does not rescue a policy that may be used to discriminate against plaintiffs based on disagreement with their views.

III.

Defendants also argue that the policy was not an effort to restrict directors' individual expression, but rather was designed to regulate the speech of directors when they were speaking on behalf of RTD. We reject this argument.

When the government designates someone to speak for it, it is free to regulate the content of that speech. However, such viewpoint-based restrictions are not allowed when the government does not itself speak, but rather, expends funds to allow others to speak. *Rosenberger v. Rector & Visitors of Univ. of Va., supra.*

Here, while RTD may regulate the speech of those who speak on its behalf as an organization, as defendants themselves have repeatedly called to our attention, plaintiffs admit that their correspondence was not intended to represent the position of RTD as a whole.

Using that admission as a rationale for rejecting the correspondence, defendants urge that the policy not only regulates the speech of those who speak for it, but also forbids any communication by directors when they are not speaking on RTD's behalf. Such a prohibition may not only run afoul of the rationale of *Bond* in that it restricts the ability of elected officials to criticize the government, but it also runs counter to a 1997 directive passed by the board. The directive, entitled "Regarding who may speak for the RTD Board," specifically authorizes directors to issue communications reflecting their own views, provided that they do not give the impression that they are speaking for the board as a whole. The directive instructs directors to use RTD letterhead designating the individual director when sending such individual correspondence.

The implication of the directive is that directors are entitled to use RTD resources when issuing such communications. The resource policy, issued personally by Tonsing as chair, would violate the terms of that directive if interpreted to proscribe all such director communications.

Defendants also point to another 1997 directive concerning the issuance of news releases. That directive limits the use of RTD resources in the preparation of news releases to those disseminated by the Chief Public Affairs Officer, and specifically prohibits directors from using RTD resources to issue personal news releases. But, that directive is limited to the issuance of news releases and does not limit the use of RTD resources for other correspondence. Defendants have not alleged that the correspondence at issue here, all of which is directed to individual recipients, consists solely of news releases.

Taken as a whole, defendants' argument that the policy concerns RTD's effort to regulate who will speak on its behalf is not supported by the undisputed facts, and does not alter the asserted fact that the policy was applied to regulate plaintiffs' speech, which all parties agree was not made on behalf of RTD.

IV.

Plaintiffs additionally contend that the policy and its application against them represent a form of retaliation for the exercise of their right to freedom of speech. They again assert there are genuine issues of material fact that preclude summary judgment on this claim. As before, we agree in part.

The government may not punish individuals for exercising their fundamental rights. *Rankin v. McPherson, supra; Ridgeway v. Kiowa Sch. Dist. C-2, supra.*

The trial court concluded that the application of the resource policy itself could not suffice as an act of retaliation. However, nothing in the law prevents the conclusion that a regulation attacked on First Amendment grounds can also be an act of retaliation against individuals for exercising their First Amendment rights.

The assertion that a government official acted to retaliate, when disputed, raises a material issue of fact. Because plaintiffs' affidavits raise the issue of retaliation through the policy, and plaintiffs have alleged that Tonsing instituted the policy to silence them, summary judgment on this issue in favor of defendants cannot stand.

Plaintiffs additionally have alleged that Tonsing made racially biased remarks to Holliday, who is African-American, and denied reimbursement of portions of her expenses. However, plaintiffs have not pleaded a claim based on racial discrimination. Under the undisputed facts, any racially biased statements Tonsing may have made (which he denies) were motivated by personal racial bias and did not consist of a form of retaliation for plaintiffs' exercise of their First Amendment rights.

The denial of reimbursement of expenses is another matter,

however. The trial court concluded that the accusation of racial bias was linked to the denial of reimbursement and therefore that both were unrelated to plaintiffs' exercise of their right to freedom of speech. A close review of plaintiffs' affidavits reveals that plaintiffs do not expressly link the denial of reimbursement of expenses to the chair's alleged racially biased remarks.

In any event, however, we must resolve all doubts concerning the asserted facts in plaintiffs' favor. *See Aspen Wilderness Workshop, Inc. v. Colo. Water Conservation Bd., supra.* Holliday's assertion is that the chair denied reimbursement of her expenses as a means of retaliating against her exercise of First Amendment rights. Tonsing, in his affidavit, denies that he has refused to grant reimbursement in retaliation.

This disputed issue of material fact independently precludes the entry of summary judgment on the claim that defendants retaliated against Holliday for exercising her First Amendment rights.

V.

Next, plaintiffs contend that the trial court erred in dismissing their claims against defendant Bergman in her official and individual capacity and against RTD arising from Bergman's actions. We agree that the dismissal cannot stand.

Bergman and RTD's motion to dismiss was considered by the trial court in conjunction with the motion for summary judgment. The trial court did not separately address the motion to dismiss in its order, except to indicate that it was treating the motion as a motion for summary judgment pursuant to C.R.C.P. 12 and 56. Hence, as with defendants' other motion for summary judgment, our review of this motion is de novo. *See Aspen Wilderness Workshop, Inc. v. Colo. Water Conservation Bd., supra.*

A.

Concerning the claim against Bergman in her official capacity, we note that government officials may be sued in their official capacities, but such suits are treated as suits against the entity. There is no difference between suing a state employee in his or her official capacity and suing the state. *See Will v. Mich. Dep't of State Police*, 491 U.S. 58, 109 S.Ct. 2304, 105 L.Ed.2d 45 (1989); *State v. Nieto*, 993 P.2d 493 (Colo. 2000).

Governmental entities subject to suit under 42 U.S.C. § 1983 may be held liable where an unconstitutional action implements or executes the official policy of the entity. However, such governmental entities cannot be held vicariously responsible under a theory of respondeat superior for the unauthorized acts of employees. *Monell v. Dep't of Soc. Serv.*, 436 U.S. 658, 98 S.Ct. 2018, 56 L.Ed.2d 611 (1978); *County of Adams v. Hibbard, 918 P.2d 212* (Colo. 1996).

Here, RTD concedes that the resource policy promulgated by Tonsing is official policy. Therefore, if Bergman executed the official policy set by Tonsing when she rejected plaintiffs' letters, and if that rejection was an unconstitutional abridgment of plaintiffs' freedom of speech, then the causal link between RTD's official policy and the unconstitutional act can be established, and RTD can be held liable directly, not vicariously, for the violation. *See County of Adams v. Hibbard, supra.*

To the extent RTD argues that it cannot be held liable for Bergman's actions in carrying out the policy because she herself was not in a policymaking position, we reject the argument.

Bergman need not be a policymaker for RTD to be liable for her actions. *See Pembaur v. City of Cincinnati*, 475 U.S. 469, 106 S.Ct. 1292, 89 L.Ed.2d 452 (1986) (county may be held liable for actions of deputy sheriffs in carrying out county prosecutor's policy). Indeed, RTD does not contend that Bergman departed from the resource policy and acted independently in reviewing plaintiffs' correspondence. To the contrary, RTD insists that Bergman at all times acted subject to Tonsing's policy and supervision.

Accordingly, this case is unlike Hibbard, but like other cases under 42 U.S.C. § 1983 in which a government official executes a directive created by a superior with policymaking authority. In such cases, the governmental entity is directly responsible for the official act of making the policy, and for the execution of the policy that follows, whether or not the employee who actually executed it was a policymaker.

Hence, the dismissal of claims against Bergman in her official capacity, and against RTD arising from Bergman's actions, was erroneous.

B.

With respect to Bergman individually, the parties agree that individuals may be personally liable under 42 U.S.C. § 1983 for acts under color of law that are not subject to qualified immunity and result in a violation of civil rights. *County of Adams v. Hibbard, supra.*

Qualified immunity is generally available to government officials in the exercise of discretionary functions, but does not apply when an official violates clearly established constitutional rights of which a reasonable person would have known. When, as here, guiding and controlling principles of the First Amendment are clearly established, a government official will not be protected by qualified immunity for acts that the official would be expected to know violate constitutional protections. *See County of Adams v. Hibbard, supra.*

Here, plaintiffs' complaint and affidavits assert that Bergman took actions to restrict their speech by rejecting correspondence they submitted for typing. Moreover, plaintiffs' assertion that Bergman stated to them that the purpose of the resource policy was the suppression of their speech sufficiently alleges her knowledge that her actions were a violation of plaintiffs' constitutional rights.

Defendants' admissions, taken together with plaintiffs' assertions concerning the statements made by Bergman to the effect that she would not allow criticism of RTD to be disseminated, establish that there is a material issue of fact regarding whether Bergman was acting at the direction of Tonsing or independently.

Accordingly, the summary judgment as to the claims against Bergman in both capacities and against RTD for her actions cannot stand.

VI.

To the extent that RTD asserts that Bergman was not a policymaker and that, therefore, it cannot be held liable for her actions as such, we agree.

Whether a governmental official is a policymaker in a particular area is a question of state law. County of Adams v. Hibbard, supra (citing City of St. Louis v. Praprotnik, 485 U.S. 112, 108 S.Ct. 915, 99 L.Ed.2d 107 (1988); Pembaur v. City of Cincinnati, 475 U.S. 469, 106 S.Ct. 1292, 89 L.Ed.2d 452 (1986)).

In Hibbard, the county took action to enforce its own zoning ordinance against the plaintiff. The county attorney, in a departure from the dictates of the ordinance, directed the demolition of a residence on plaintiff's property. The court concluded that the departure from the ordinance broke the causal link between the county's enactment of the ordinance and the unconstitutional act of destroying the building, and therefore the county would not be liable for such action. Additionally, because the county attorney was not in a position to make county policy concerning zoning, his independent decision could not create direct liability for the county. Here, the law reserves policymaking authority to the board. See § 32-9-109.5(4), C.R.S. 2001. As further discussed below, the RTD by-laws authorized Tonsing as the chair to make policy with respect to the use of RTD staff. Accordingly, Bergman, as the board executive assistant, has no policymaking authority.However, RTD does not contend that Bergman was acting on her own in rejecting plaintiffs' correspondence. In fact, it has consistently asserted that she was acting pursuant to Tonsing's official policy. Accordingly, any liability imposed here will necessarily not result from Bergman's actions as a policymaker.

VII.

To the extent that plaintiffs contend that the chair, Tonsing, lacked authority to institute the resource policy, we reject that contention.

The RTD by-laws authorize the chair to supervise and give day-to-day direction to the board executive assistant. The job description of the board executive assistant includes management of office staff and resources.

Thus, the chair was authorized to control the use of staff resources and to promulgate policy regarding their use.

VIII.

Defendants contend that Mary Blue, though denominated as a party to this appeal by plaintiffs, is not properly a party because the trial court denied, as moot, plaintiffs' motion to add her as a party. Because we reverse the judgment that rendered that motion moot, we direct the trial court to reconsider the motion to add Blue as a defendant.

Finally, also in view of our disposition, we do not address plaintiffs' vagueness challenge to the resource policy. The trial court may revisit this claim if plaintiffs again raise it on remand.

We need not address plaintiffs' remaining contentions.

The judgment is reversed, and the case is remanded to the trial court with directions to reconsider the motion to add Mary Blue as a party defendant and to proceed with the consideration of plaintiffs' claims.

JUDGE VOGT and JUDGE CRISWELL concur.

APPENDIX F

2002
SENATE JOINT RESOLUTION 02-044

BY SENATOR(S) Andrews, Arnold, Cairns, Chlouber, Dyer, Epps, Evans, Gordon, Hagedorn, Hernandez, Hillman, Lamborn, May, Musgrave, Nichol, Owen, Taylor, Teck, Anderson, Fitz-Gerald, Hanna, Isgar, Linkhart, Matsunaka, McElhany, Pascoe, Perlmutter, Phillips, Reeves, Takis, Tate, Thiebaut, Tupa, and Windels, also REP-RESENTATIVE(S) Mitchell, Clapp, Decker, Groff, Harvey, Johnson, Stafford, Williams T., Coleman, and Young.

CONCERNING THE SUPPORT OF THE GENERAL ASSEMBLY FOR CONSTITUTIONAL PROTECTIONS ACCORDED ELECTED OFFICIALS IN EXPRESSING THEIR VIEWS ON PUBLIC ISSUES.

WHEREAS, On September 27, 2001, the Colorado Court of Appeals rendered a decision in the case of *Holliday v. Regional Transportation District*, Court of Appeals No. OOCA1778 (Colo. App. 2001), ordering the trial court to proceed with considera-tion of claims by two Regional Transportation District (RTD) directors, Gloria Holliday and Jack McCroskey, that their free speech rights were denied and their federal civil rights violated by RTD's policy denying the directors access to RTD resources to disseminate correspondence unfavorable to RTD; and

WHEREAS, On April 15, 2002, the Colorado Supreme Court denied RTD's petition for certiorari, making the Court of Appeals' decision the final judicial pronouncement in the case at this time; and

WHEREAS, The Court of Appeals' decision in *Holliday* announces principles relating to the acceptable justifications for government involvement in abridgement of protected speech in public and nonpublic forums, and

WHEREAS, The *Holliday* decision reviewed the content and implementation of an RTD policy denying the plaintiffs access to staff assistance and materials, specifically, the withholding of typing services for correspondence to state officials and news media containing criticism of RTD.

WHEREAS, The Colorado General Assembly is the legislative department of the state of Colorado, vested with the legislative power of the state, and its deliberations on disputed public issues that come before it demonstrate on a daily basis that "speech concerning public affairs is more than self-expression; it is the essence of self-government."; and

WHEREAS, The Colorado General Assembly serves as a model for all deliberative legislative bodies in this state and should observe constitutional protections accorded core political speech engaged in by elected officials that necessitate the absolute avoidance of viewpoint discrimination and regulation of speech based on its substantive content or the message it conveys, now, therefore,

Be It Resolved by the Senate of the Sixty-third General Assembly of the State of Colorado, the House of Representatives concurring herein:

That the General Assembly expresses its full support and endorsement of the principles of free speech announced by the Colorado Court of Appeals in the case of *Holliday v. Regional Transportation District*, especially as those principles relate to prohibiting viewpoint discrimination, allowing elected officials the widest latitude to express their views on issues of policy, and promoting the free discussion of important policy differences that directly affect the public. The General Assembly further recommends other legislative bodies of the state accord the free speech rights of their own elected officials the highest degree of protection consistent with the United States and Colorado Constitutions.

_____   _____
Stan Matsunaka   Doug Dean
PRESIDENT OF   SPEAKER OF THE HOUSE
THE SENATE   OF REPRESENTATIVES

_____   _____
Karen Goldman   Judith Rodrigue
SECRETARY OF   CHIEF CLERK OF THE HOUSE
THE SENATE   OF REPRESENTATIVES

PAGE 2-SENATE JOINT RESOLUTION 02-044